GW01149680

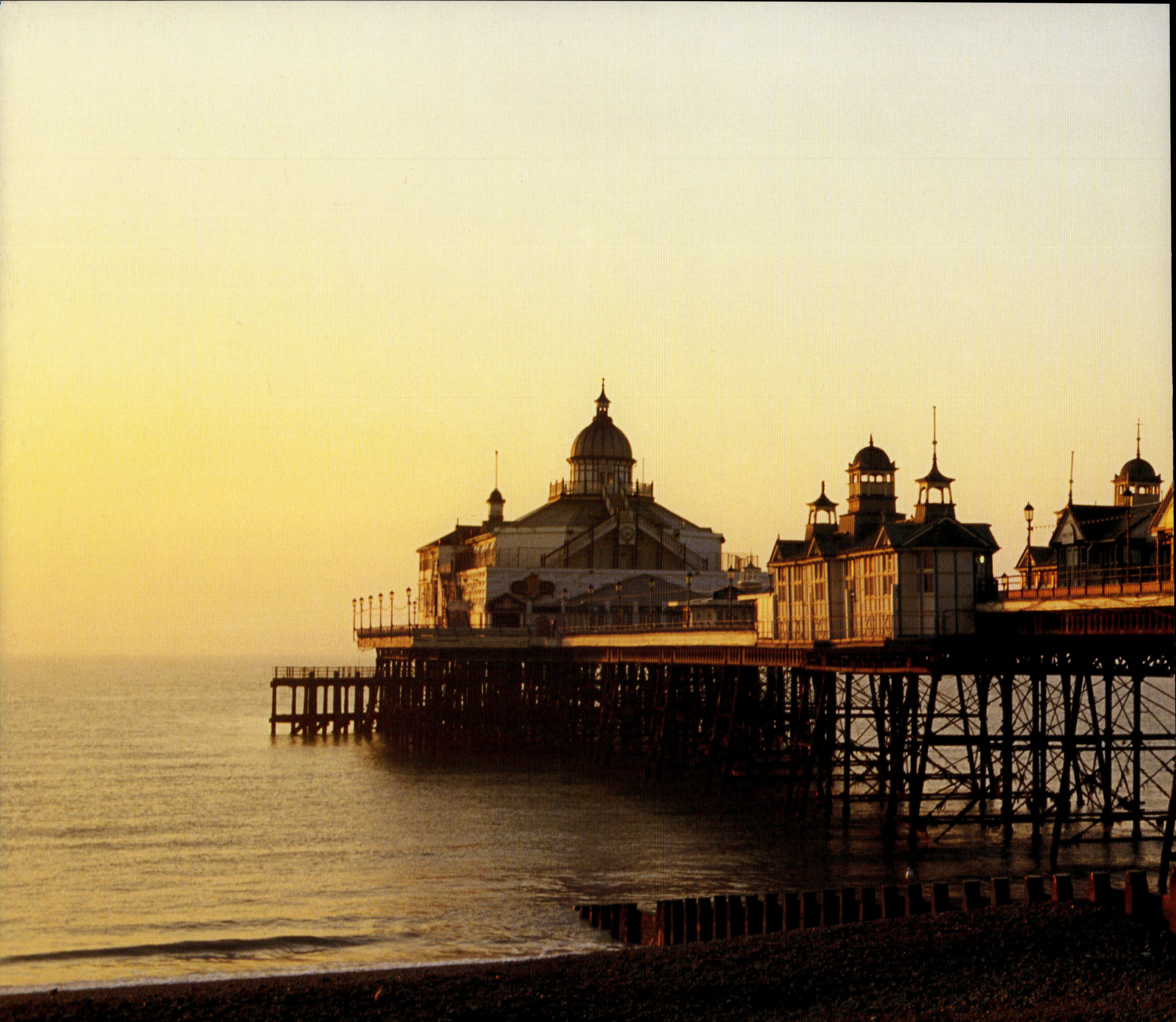

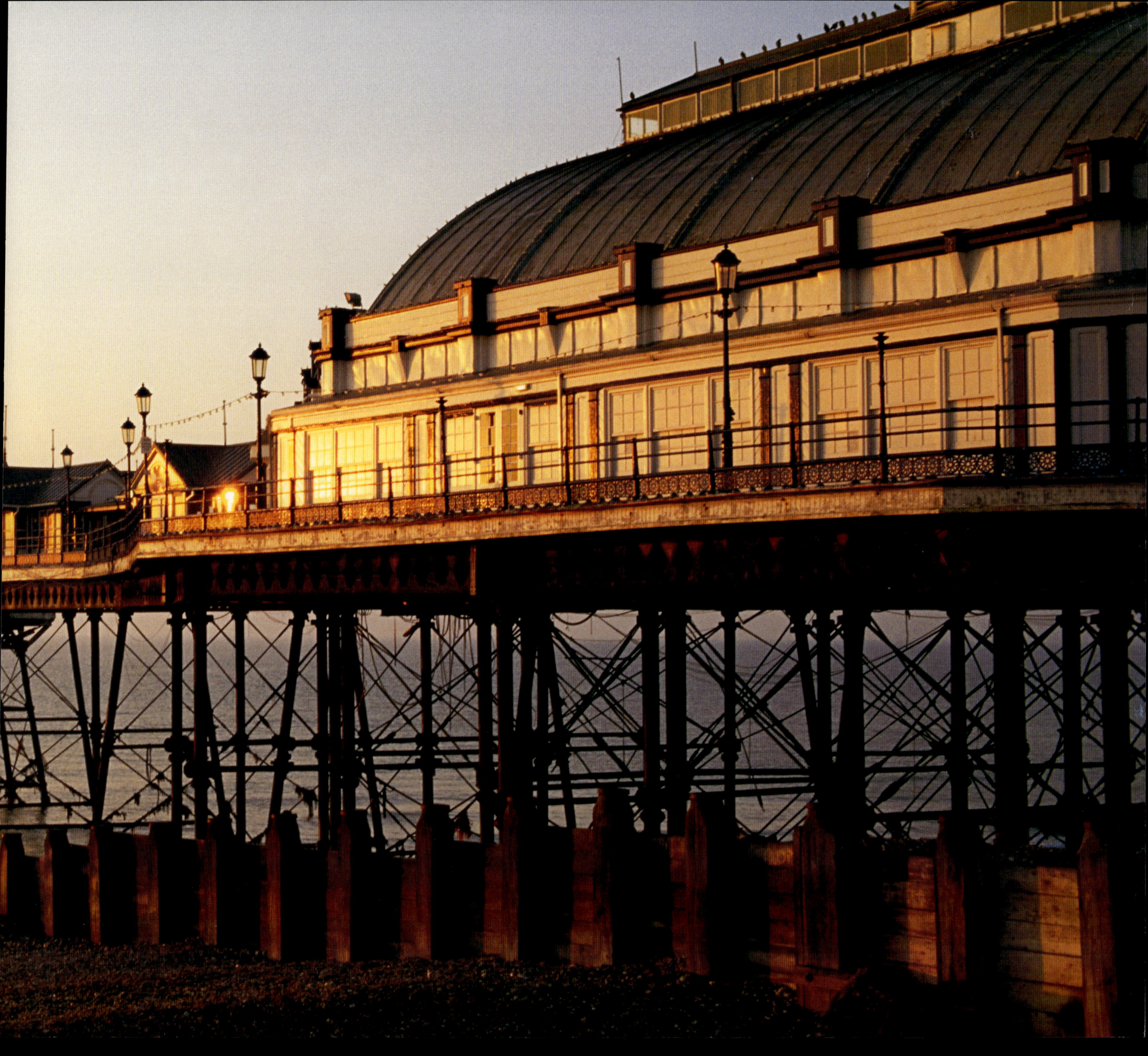

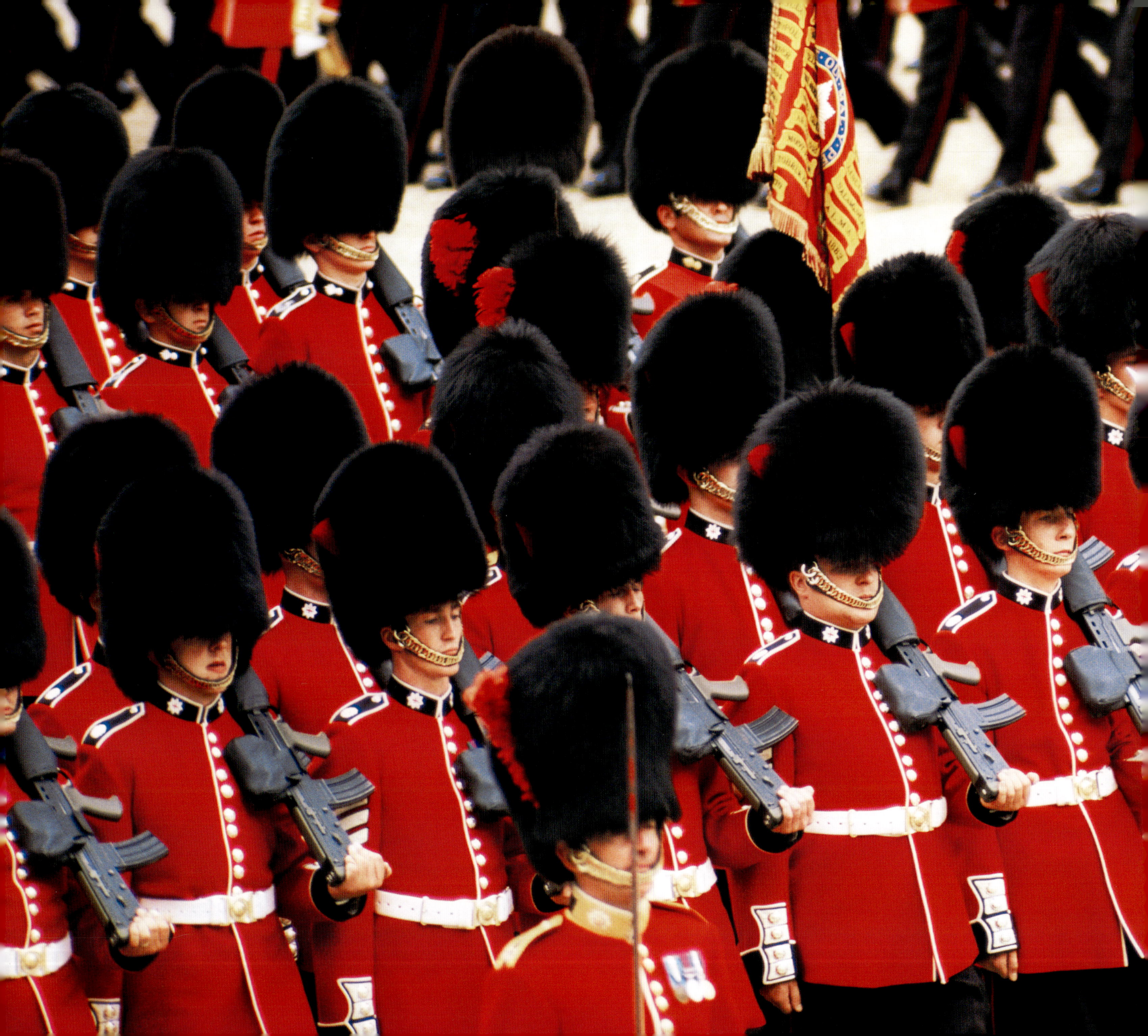

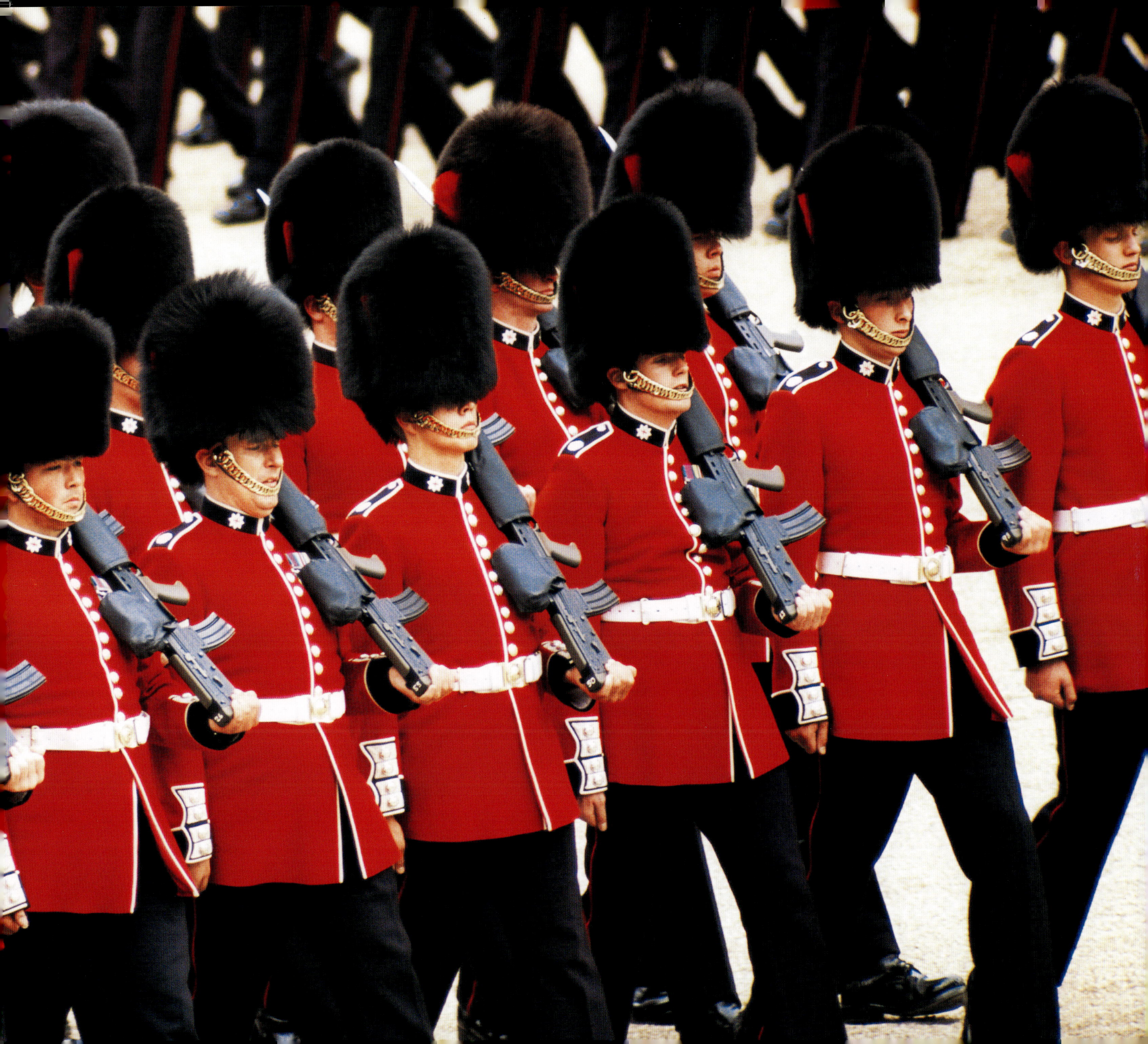

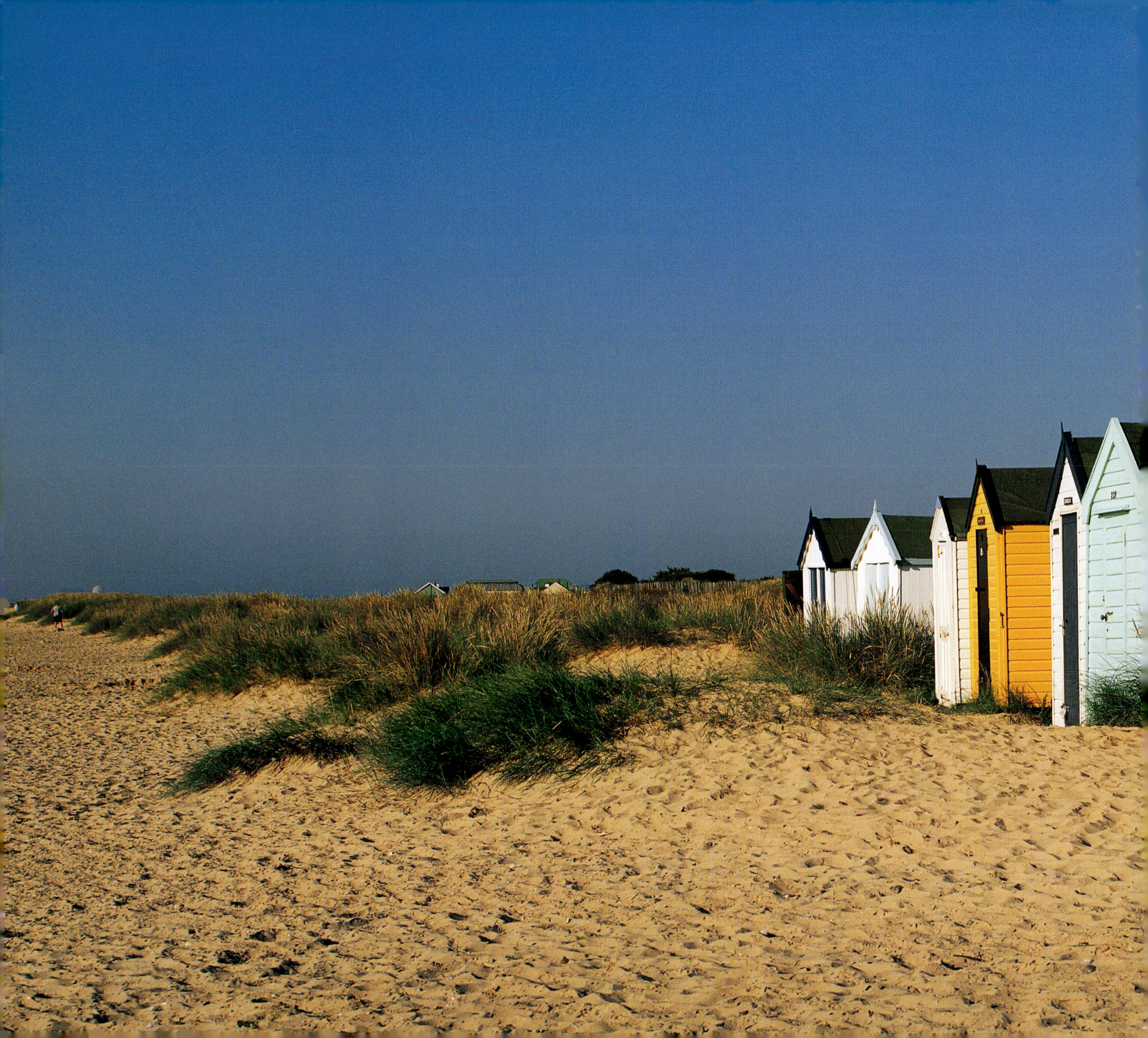

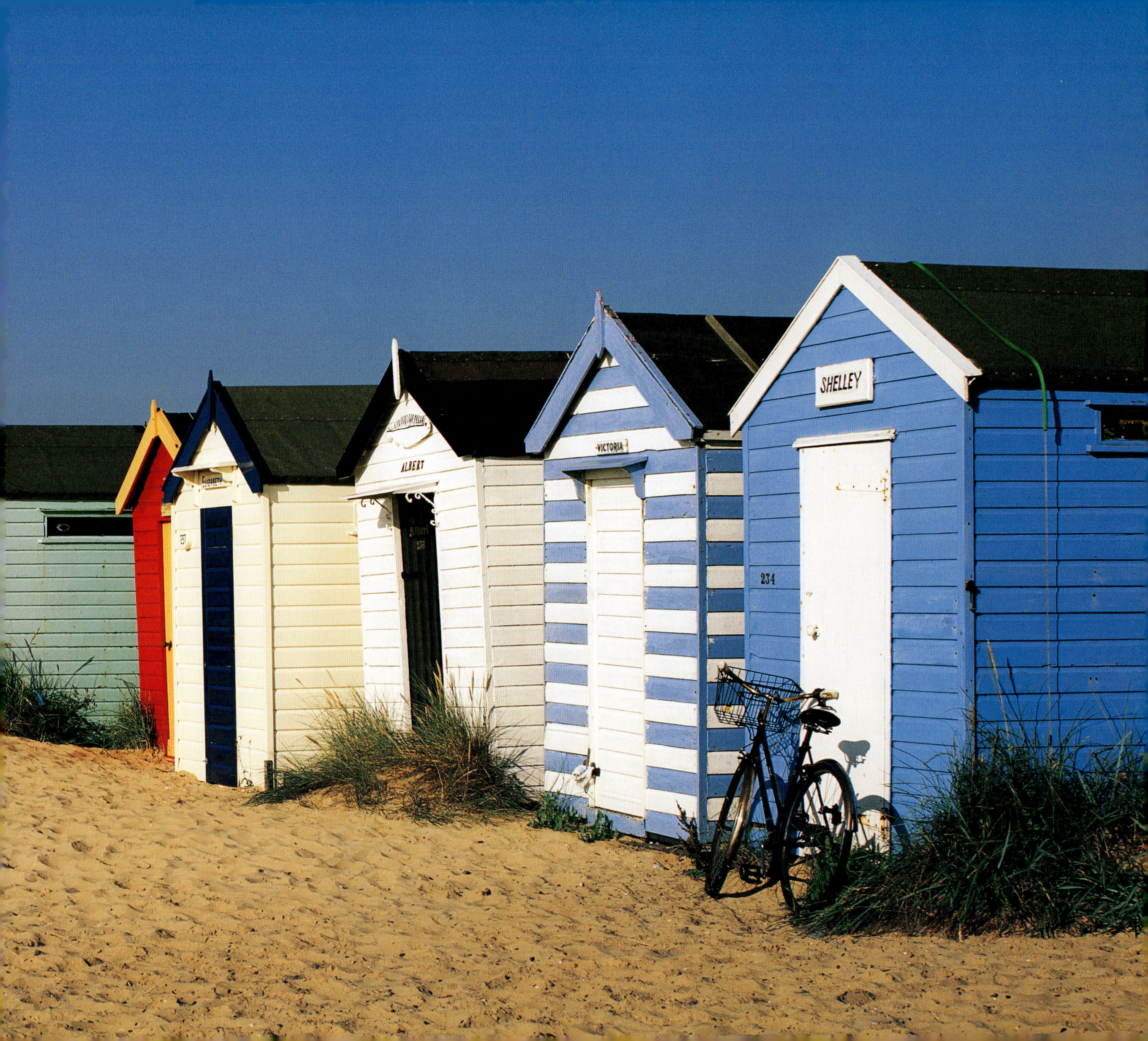
ALBERT
VICTORIA
SHELLEY
234

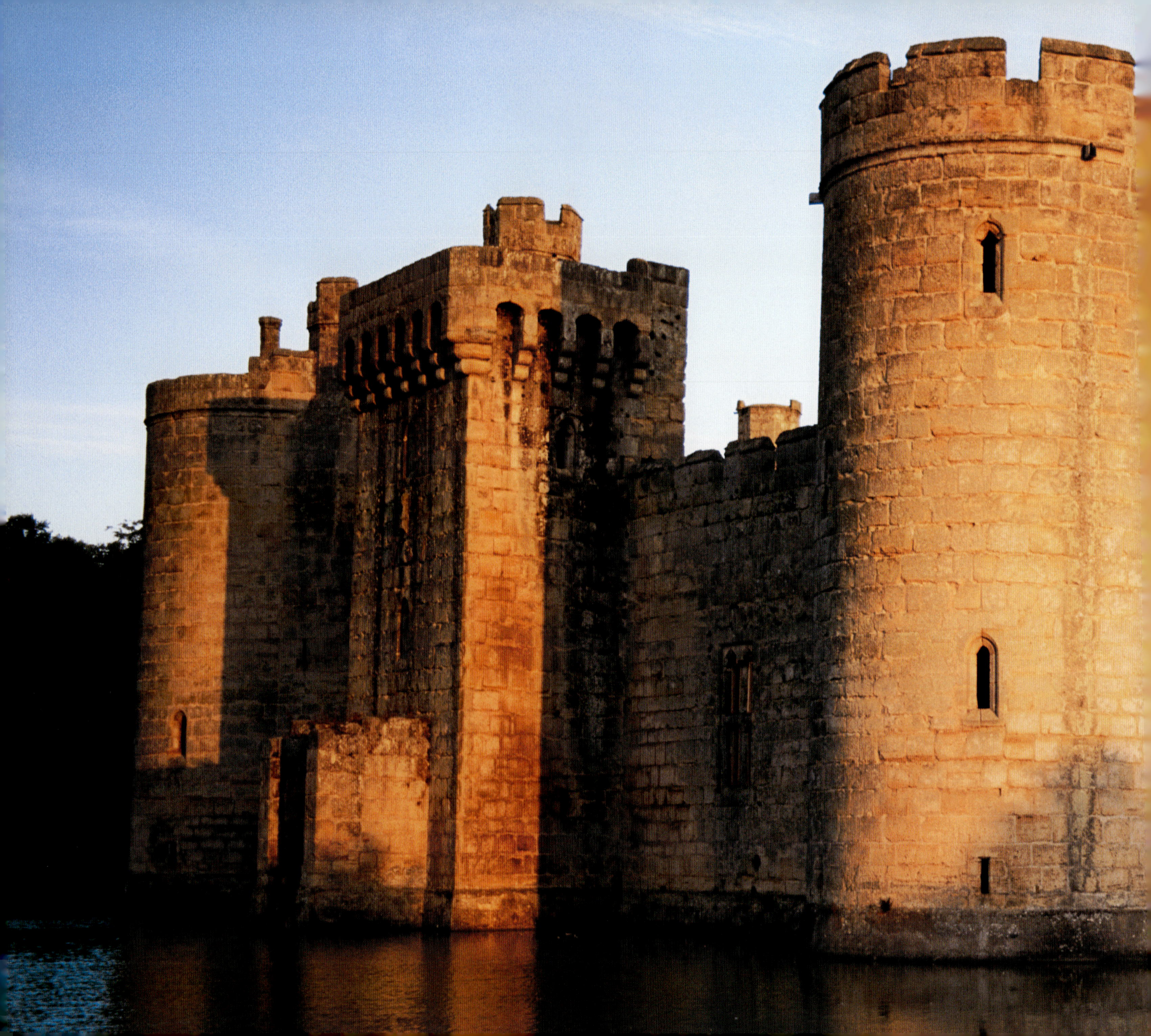

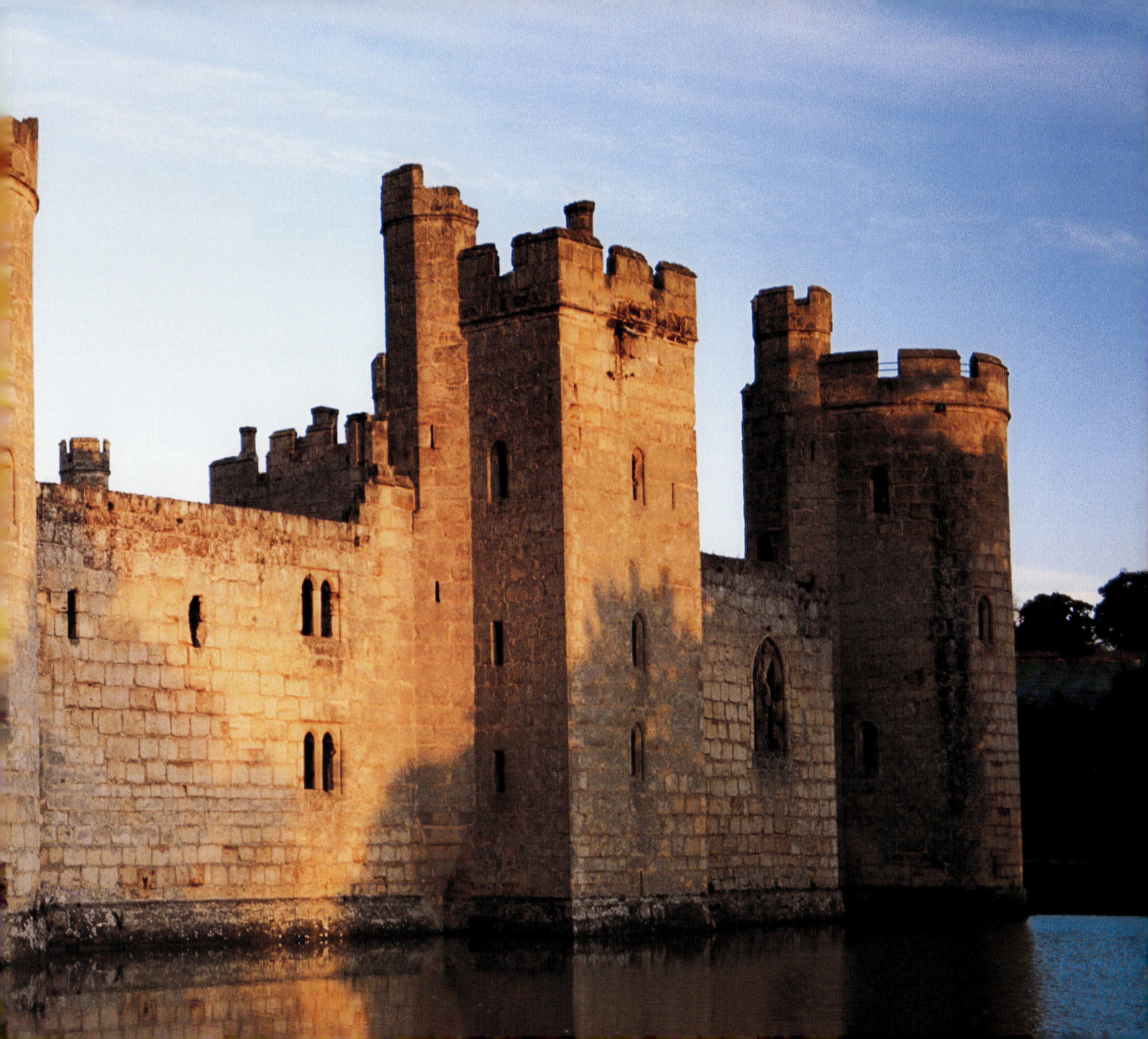

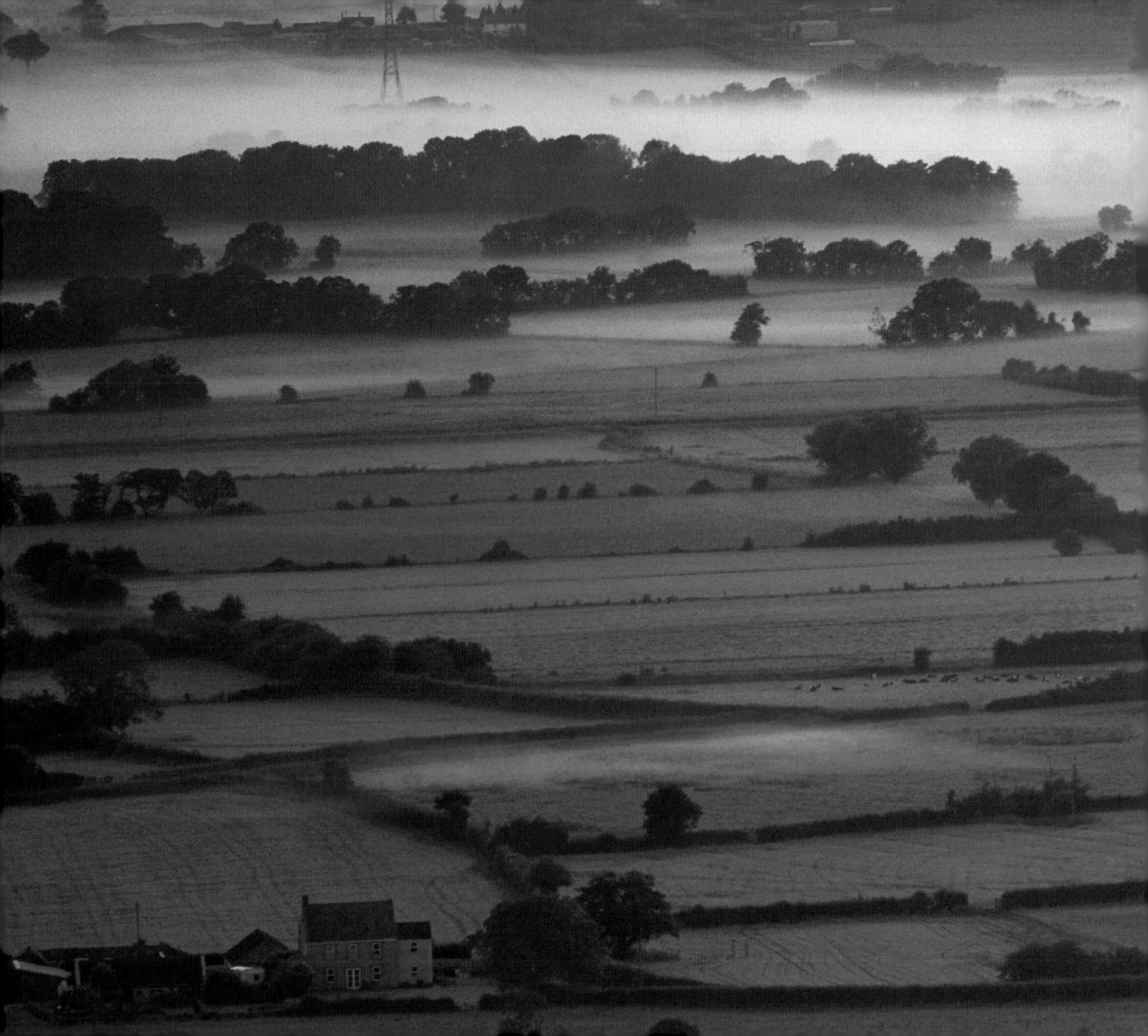

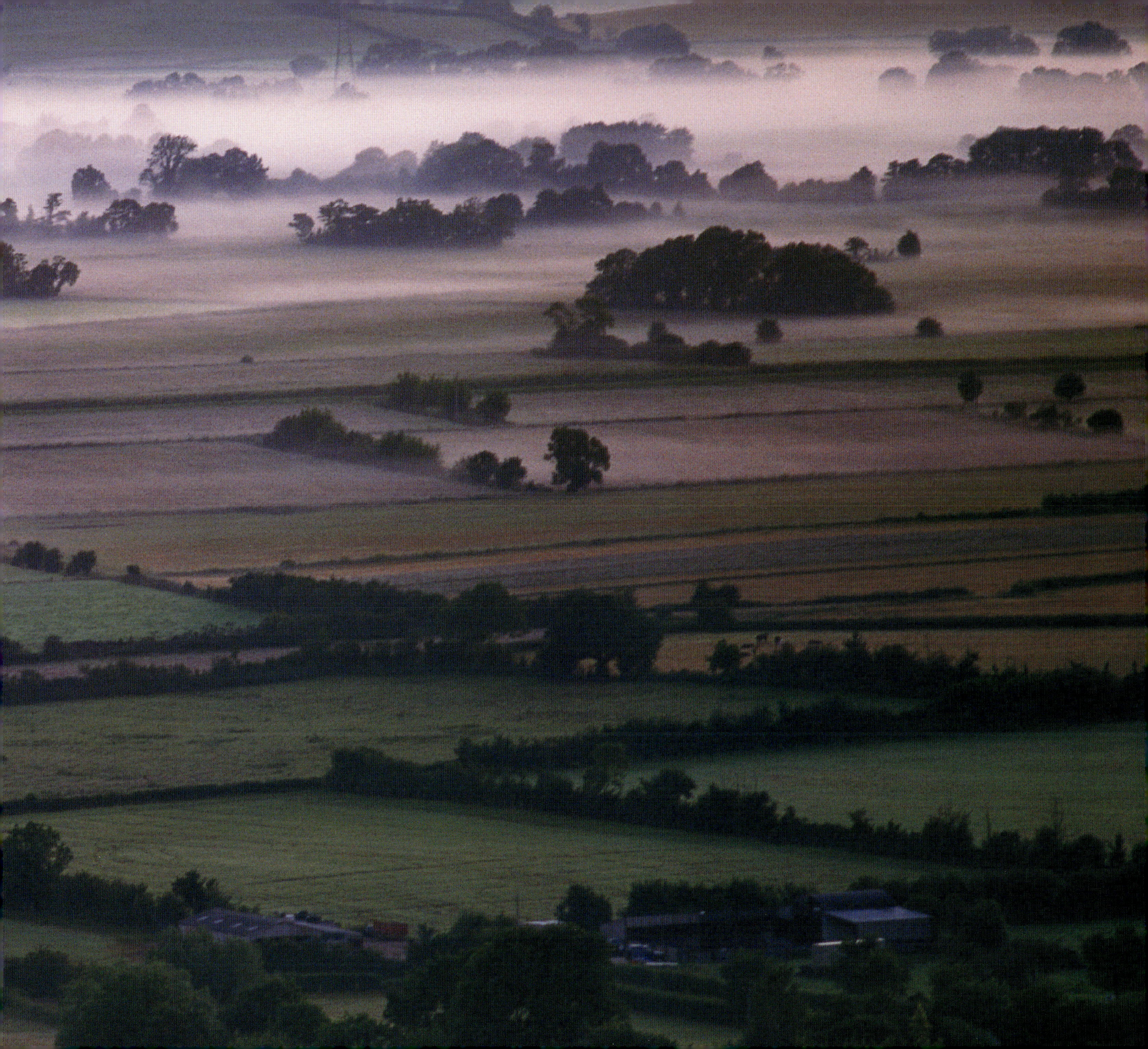

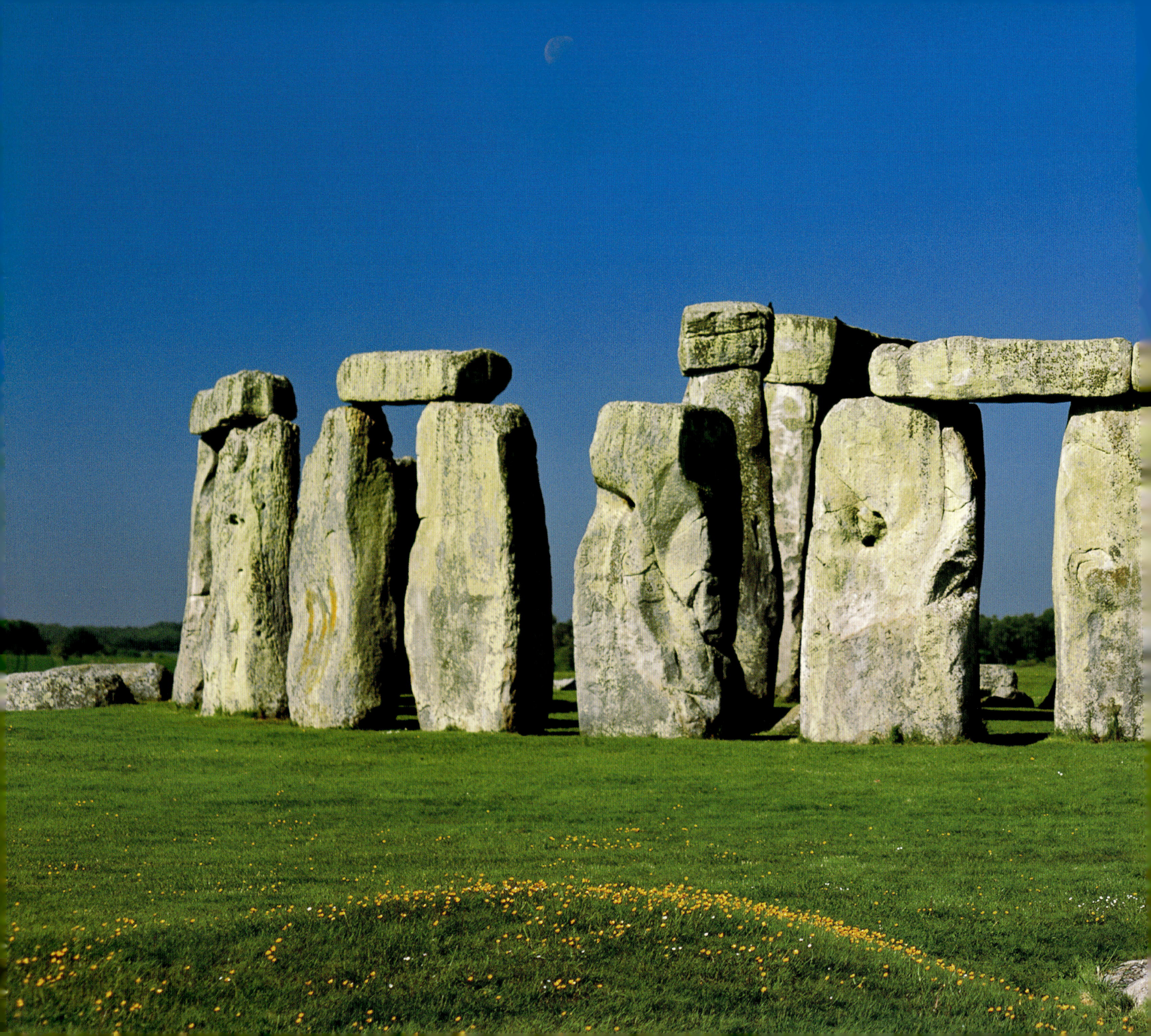

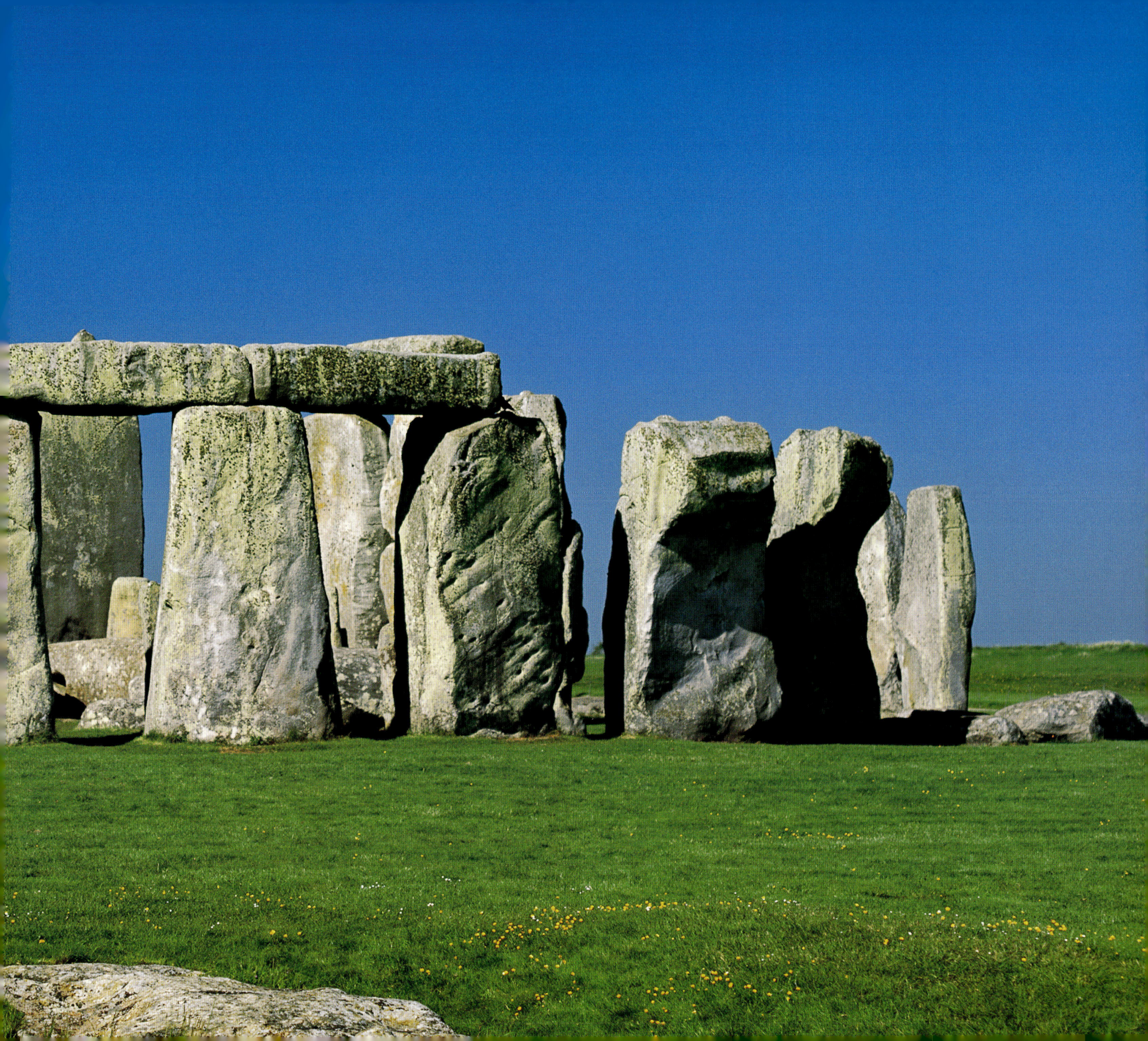

YE OLDE
ROBIN HOOD INN
THE PROSPECT OF WHITBY
SHAKESPEARE'S HEAD
LONDON
THE SHERLOCK HOLMES
WHITBREAD
THE CROOKED SURGEC
FULLER'S
THE BANKER
The Celebrated
LD KING'S HEA
Est.1881
SMUGGLERS
HOTEL
EST.1873
THE BEAR & STAFF
COACH & HORSES
THE CRICKETERS
DUNCTON
W.G. GRACE of ENGLAND 1848-1915
HOUSE
THE DOG AND DUCK
BRICKLAYERS ARMS
The
MARKET PORTER
BEACHY HEAD

PORTRAIT OF ENGLAND

STEVE VIDLER
TEXT BY DAVID WATTS

DAIICHI
DAIICHI PUBLISHERS

Published by Daiichi Publishers Co. Ltd.
20–22 8/F, Zung Fu Ind. Bldg.
1067 King's Road, Quarry Bay
Hong Kong

Tel: (852) 2893 1236
Fax: (852) 2343 4946
Email: dip@daiichipublishers.com
www.daiichipublishers.com

Photography by Steve Vidler
Text by David Watts
Book design by Catherine Lutman

Photographs and text copyright © 2008

All rights reserved.

No part of this book may be transmitted in any form, or by any means, electronic, mechanical, photocopying or otherwise, without the prior permission of Daiichi Publishers Co. Ltd.

Printed in China.

ISBN 978-988-99143-5-6

FOREWORD	19
LONDON	22
THE SOUTH	48
THE SOUTH WEST	78
CENTRAL ENGLAND	102
EASTERN ENGLAND	114
THE NORTH	126

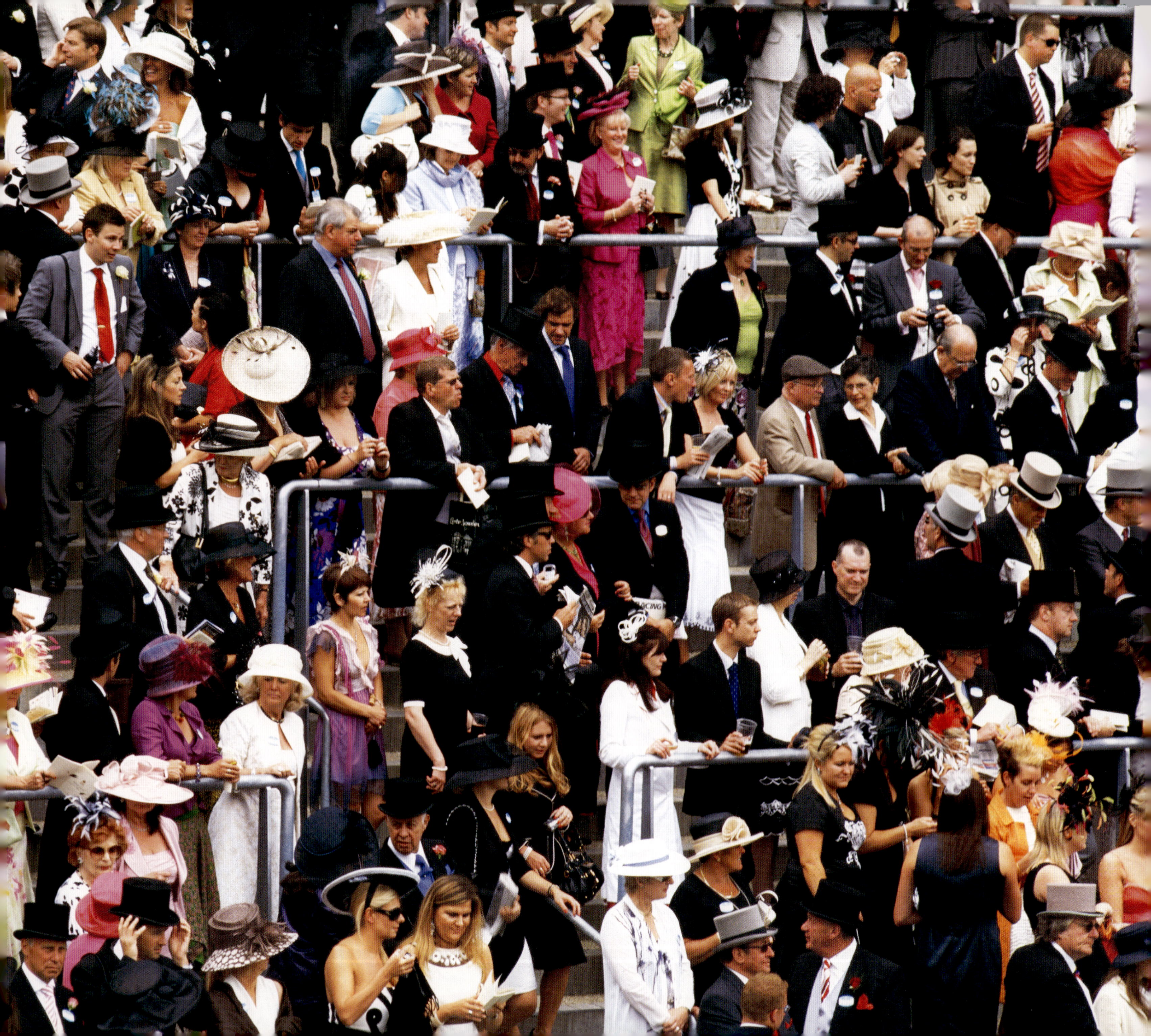

FOREWORD

There are many Englands that epitomise this ancient island: the skylark in a powder-blue sky celebrating summer above the South Downs; the wind-blown ruggedness of the Yorkshire Moors or the winding lanes and cosy pubs of Devon.

The landscape, soft and rural, harsh and industrial by turns, has remained remarkably untouched by the passing centuries from the 'garden of England' in Kent to the Midlands and North-West.

Just as her people made the country into a great trading nation by travelling to the four corners of the earth so she has now become a world focal point: the original home of sports that now span the globe from soccer to golf and cricket. But underneath the modern economic clothing, England and its landscape and people remain much as they always were: protective of island life in a green and pleasant land. Sometimes that might make them seem a little narrow minded but it means a countryside which has escaped the blights of advertising, excessive marketing and over-development.

So arm yourselves with those three cardinal assets of the native Brits: fortitude, patience and a sense of humour and brave the transport system to get at the real England. Remember, you can make a lot of friendships in queues. Britain may have invented the modern railway network but somewhere along the way governments forgot what a great idea it was so they are now having to re-learn its virtues.

There is a lot to see out there whatever your interests: dozens of exquisite cathedrals and churches, numerous castles and palaces, country houses, museums and gardens; broad acres of agricultural land, moor land and vale; majestic rivers and woodland. Don't confine yourself to those landmarks within easy reach of London such as Blenheim; every region of Britain has its share of great houses while Yorkshire has another 38 majestic mansions even after you have seen the gems of Castle Howard and Harewood House.

Once you are in your locale of choice get away from the obvious, and stay away from the traffic clogged motorways and major roads. Staying at a local bed and breakfast will bring you a level of understanding, involvement and enjoyment unattainable any other way. Strike it lucky and your hostess will have you returning time and again to relive that first encounter with the glories of Gloucestershire, sitting down to enjoy a summer tea on the green at Bourton-on-the-Water; or climbing the Cat Bells to eat a picnic on the steep incline overlooking Windermere in the Lake District. Stand alongside Hadrian's Wall and soak up the isolation and wild drama of Northumbria's border country. Here it is easy to imagine being posted as a Roman soldier slapping your arms against your body to keep warm, pining for the warmth of Naples, while facing the grim reality of keeping out the hostile hooligans from north of the border.

While you're contemplating Hadrian and all his works there is a perfect opportunity to travel to the eastern most end of the wall to the picturesque border town of Alnwick. The castle is an idyllic place to spend a day not only because of the famously redeveloped garden but because the castle has played a prominent role as a location for the Harry Potter films.

Each region will reward frequent visits: moving out from the capital to the south and south east Kent's fruit orchards and even wineries are matched with its winding lanes and friendly villages. Stand on the cliffs east of Dover on a clear day and the French coast will seem so close you could reach out and touch it, the ferries arcing back and forth across the busiest sea lanes in the world look like lines of sugar icing on a deep blue cake. The trim Dover-Folkestone Heritage coastal highway carries you on to the Romney Marshes and Rye as the countryside gives way to Sussex and its unmatched coast, its picture-perfect white cliffs and some of the longest hours of sunshine in the country.

The broad hinterland of the Sussex Downs provides a backdrop to the unwinding coast on to the ancient region of Wessex. As an introduction to this beautiful stretch of the country a visit to placid Lulworth Cove, a perfect crescent-shaped haven for small boats contrasting with the dramatic foreland of Durdle Door nearby but do yourself a favour and do not try to swim through the 'door' — it has a vicious ocean undertow. Contrasting with the drama of the coast the precipitous 18th century Gold Hill in the town of Shaftesbury, which has helped sell many a loaf of bread through television advertising over the years, is a pacific relief.

Neo-classical Bath with the elegant sweep of its Palladian terraces mark it out as one of Europe's most memorable cities and reinforce the value of England's determination to conserve. It is an important part of any visit to the south-west contrasting, as it does, with the wind-swept wastes of heath-covered Exmoor, wild and bracing which, along with Dartmoor, gives a strong sense of the face of the country before widespread human settlement.

The Lake District is quintessentially English: it features the closest thing the country has to mountains: a seemingly placid range of rounded hills set by lakes that can be deceptively tranquil but erupt in violent rain storms in short order; a very English soft-focus version of the Alps without the hard edges. Whatever the weather this is the place to enjoy walks — a long perambulation round Buttermere interrupted by dogs racing to the top of the fell at breathtaking speeds-visions that will open up vistas almost unchanged for millennia. It is a dramatic counterpoint to the cosy Hill Top farm house at Near Sawrey, north-west of Windermere that once made this Beatrix Potter's favourite part of the world. At any moment you expect to see Peter Rabbit peering at you from the lawn as visitors from Japan come to pay homage to an iconic author.

From the West of the country it is a wonderful, if testing, scenic drive across the backbone of England to the Yorkshire Dales. You climb up away from the M6 motorway on a switchback journey into a world where the summers are brief and the winters seem never-ending; a world where nature takes no prisoners. The narrow two-lane road winds between dry stonewalling in a landscape that has not changed for centuries. Most of the villages and small towns are untroubled by modern technology — in many places it is not possible to get a mobile telephone signal — or the dubious benefits of chain shops and no-one feels the worse off for that. The centre of Hawes on a summer Sunday morning resembles a local version of Piccadilly Circus — walkers, cyclists, riders, motor-cyclists and mere spectators meet on the green or in the clutch of pubs to prepare for the day's adventures, chatting loudly on wooden benches set beside tables on the grass.

In summer the area is a patchwork of emerald green fields intersected by moss and lichen-covered stone walls with occasional animal shelters. In winter it is one of the bleakest places in Britain with heavy falls of snow and freezing temperatures that gives rise to hardy and hospitable local people who know what it is to struggle against the elements to survive and make a living.

The area's key lifeline is the A66, double-tracked for much of its length, and one of the most dangerous roads in the country. It is dangerous because its great, open sweeping runs across the peak of England's backbone is a temptation to all drivers to overtake where there is insufficient visibility and for motor-cyclists to let rip at speeds at which the heart rules the head.

The road cascades down to one of the great, iconic turning points on the English trunk road system — the A1 at Scotch Corner — where it intersects the major trunk route from London to Edinburgh. Unfortunately the era when the Scotch Corner Hotel offered excellent food and lodging to passing horse-drawn carriages is long gone and transiting tourists would be better advised to go to the Black Bull in the nearby village of Moulton to eat before heading off to the Vale of York via the pretty market town of Northallerton.

The Black Bull illustrates the point that a journey through England no longer means one has to suffer in a culinary purgatory. The English may have lost little of their arrogance, along with the Empire, but they have certainly begun to learn from their continental neighbours how to tell well-prepared fresh food from bad and that there is no excuse for putting up with the latter. With the right good food guide in hand it should be possible to navigate from one foodie hotspot to the next just as successfully as the tourist who moves on to the next way point, the city of York.

The Vale of York in spring and summer epitomises the English countryside at its verdant, productive best: acres of rich, dark earth that produce corn and vegetables in abundance whose value is once more being appreciated as costs rise and the islands think more in terms of self-sufficiency rather than meeting the objectives of some far-off Brussels bureaucrat. York Minster, which was started in 1220 and is the second largest Gothic cathedral north of the Alps, towers over the city of York and sets the tone for this majestic place characterised by centuries of belief. But it carries its history lightly and nowhere does the visitor feel the past pressing down on them.

The County of Lincoln could not be more different from Yorkshire. To some its very flatness equates with mind-bending boredom; to others its England's 'big sky country', hundreds of thousands of open acres where the sky dominates from horizon to horizon be it in the pale blue tint of spring or the leaden skies that herald the soft rain that feeds its fertility; either way the cathedral city of Lincoln can be seen from many miles away, its majestic honey-coloured stone reminiscent of the Vatican.

Complete a circular Tour of England through Constable Country — the enchanting birthplace of John Constable, perhaps England's greatest landscape artist. The soothing greens and yellows are a restful preparation before you re-acquaint yourself with the rigours of the capital. Flatford Mill, the subject of one of his most famous paintings is little changed and you feel you might even come across him emerging from the timbered frame of the Guildhall in Lavenham.

FRONT COVER: **GREEN MEADOWS AND FELLSIDE FIELDS:** Graphic patterns formed by stone walls are symbolic of the Yorkshire Dales National Park.

PAGE 1: **THE ANGEL OF THE NORTH:** More than one person every second looks at this regional symbol of the north from the nearby A1 motorway or the east coast main railway line from London to Edinburgh.

PAGE 2–3: **VICTORIAN MARVEL:** Opened in 1872 Eastbourne Pier is built on stilts that sit in cups on the sea bed, allowing the whole structure to sway during stormy weather.

PAGE 4–5: **TROOPING THE COLOUR:** Every June Horseguards' Parade in London erupts in a sea of scarlet tunics and black bear skin head gear as the army celebrates the sovereign's birthday.

PAGE 5–6: **WE DO LIKE TO BE BESIDE THE SEASIDE:** The shabby look of a string of beach huts at Southwold in Suffolk belies their value; they can easily cost up to £40,000.

PAGE 7–8: **CHOCOLATE BOX CASTLE:** Bodiam Castle in East Sussex epitomises the classic English castle. Completed in 1388, it is now a favourite for book covers and jigsaw puzzles.

PAGE 9–10: **A SEASON OF MISTS:** Somerset is a county of ancient mystery and youthful dreams where long summer days are spent at the world famous Glastonbury music festival.

PAGE 11–12: **PUT ANOTHER STEAK ON THE BARBIE:** Before it was built in 2,500 BC the site of Stonehenge was popular for barbecues. Cattle were herded from as far away as Wales and Scotland for feasts.

PAGE 13: **ALL ENGLISH LIFE IS HERE:** The pub may be on the decline but these signs are as inventive as ever.

PAGE 17: **ELITE CROWD:** Top hats and tails are still preferred dress for race meetings at Royal Ascot.

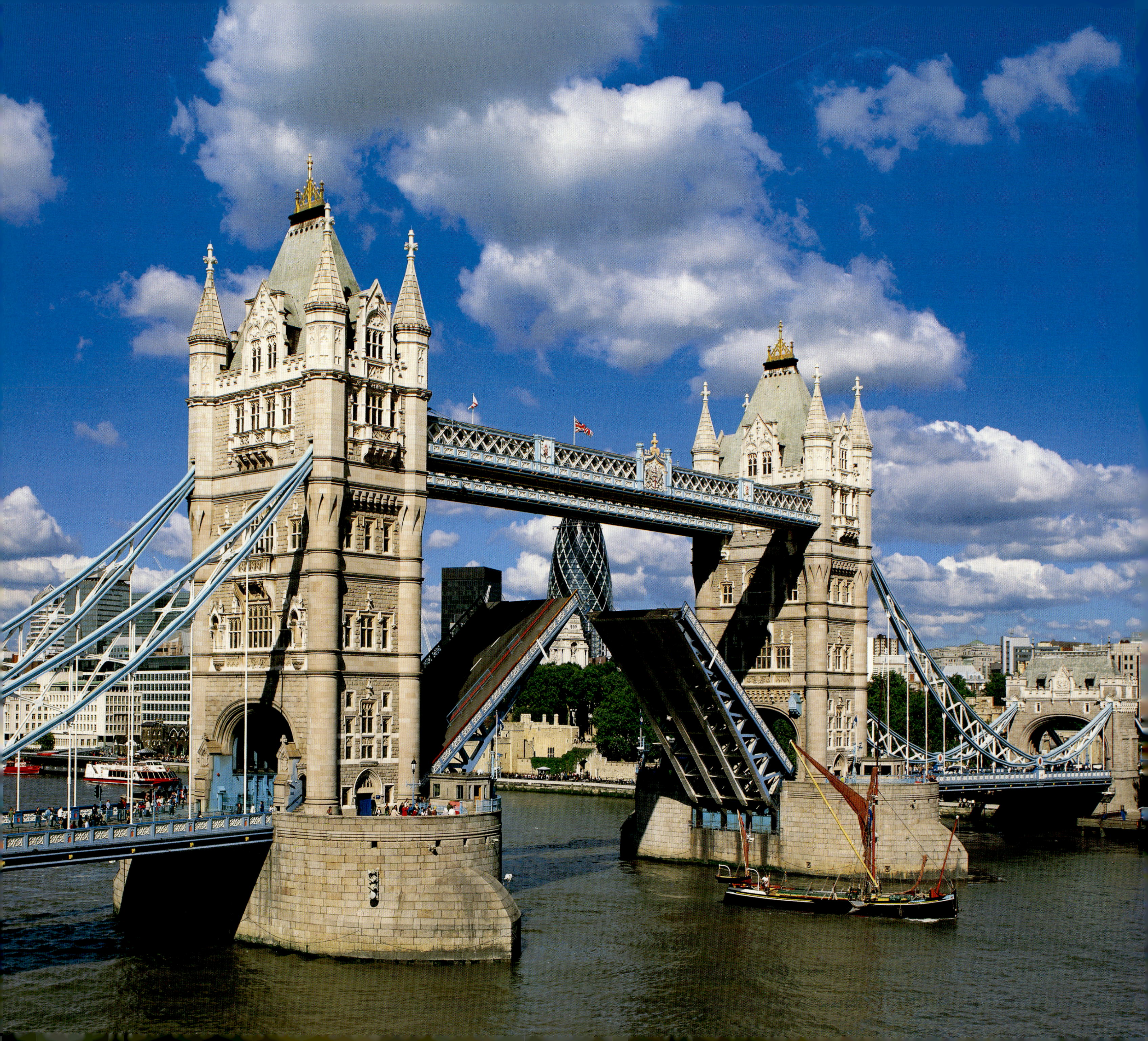

LONDON

London is a city at the centre of many worlds. For centuries it ruled an empire; now it is at the heart of the modern empires of business, finance, aviation and shipping, medicine and science. All, in turn, have shaped the city and its people. Its very diversity, with at least 300 languages spoken, has created a new linguistic and cultural empire at the heart of Europe, equidistant in time and habit between the North American continent and Asia, an electronic crossroads that keeps the worldwide worlds of business and finance turning.

But the city and its people beneath the modern persona are the same as ever they were: the same work-a-day human drive that is its life-blood; the same rich mixture of buildings makes up the cityscape (OPPOSITE PAGE) with some new and exciting additions testifying to a place and people never content with their achievements.

The same lively markets and manufacturing in food and clothes enliven the East End, only new races and generations of immigrants and refugees people the market stalls. The City of London embraces every technological trading innovation with alacrity, striving hard to stay ahead of rivals in Frankfurt and New York. Rolls-Royces and Bentleys, Porsches and Lamborghinis are the carriages of choice in the West End and Chelsea and the great sea of humanity that stretches out west towards the busiest international airport in the world at Heathrow grows more concentrated.

London's arts and theatre, music and drama is rich and varied, drawing visitors from around the world to theatres and concert halls that are international icons.

At heart of it all the Palace of Westminster and Buckingham Palace signify the truth that the more the tsunami of change swirls around the great British institutions the more they resist its tidal wave.

PORTRAIT OF ENGLAND

SENT TO THE TOWER: Her Majesty's Royal Palace and Fortress, more commonly known as the Tower of London (OPPOSITE PAGE), no longer houses enemies of the realm but still looks fearsome.

Tower Bridge, the old symbol of the capital's wealth (TOP RIGHT), frames the new city of London skyline as another hectic day draws to a close.

Two Beefeaters, the ancient guardians of the Tower (BOTTOM LEFT), compare notes on another hard day protecting the kingdom's most valued treasures, the Crown Jewels.

Legend has it that if the ravens ever leave the White Tower both the tower and the kingdom will fall (BOTTOM RIGHT).

LONDON

FULL CIRCLE: Three and a half million people a year 'fly' on the London Eye affording a view 40 kilometres in all directions on a clear day (TOP RIGHT).

Queen Victoria may not have had much time for its 'dreary' interior but St Paul's Cathedral (BOTTOM LEFT) has seen all the nation's great historic occasions since there was first a building of that name on the site in 604 AD.

(BOTTOM RIGHT) The Great Bell of Big Ben weighs 13.5 tonnes and has been tolling through events great and small since 1859, not even stopping in time of war.

It has seen some of the greatest speeches in the English language and some of the juiciest scandals but the Palace of Westminster (OPPOSITE PAGE), remains a beacon for those in search of freedom.

LONDON

PORTRAIT OF ENGLAND

NELSON'S VICTORY: Admiral Nelson's column (OPPOSITE PAGE) was built to commemorate his victory at the Battle of Trafalgar in 1805. Barbados' capital Bridgetown erected a smaller statue thirty years earlier.

(TOP LEFT): Since it was erected in 1893 the statue of Eros in Piccadilly Circus has been the nations's favourite meeting place.

Once a power station the building now houses Tate Modern (BOTTOM LEFT) the pride, and in some cases the shame, of British modern art.

Buckingham Palace (BOTTOM RIGHT), home of the British royal family and of one of the world's longest-running soap operas. The storyline may be less exciting since the death of Lady Diana but the ending is still just as unpredictable.

LONDON

INSURANCE ICON: Sir Richard Rogers' Lloyds Building (TOP LEFT), completed in 1986, epitomises the re-invigoration of London's architecture.

30 St Mary Axe (BOTTOM LEFT), nicknamed the Gherkin, makes a stark counterpoint to the traditional buildings around it in the financial heart of the City.

The office of the mayor of London is housed in surely the capital's most odd building (BOTTOM RIGHT), appearing like a tomato that's been partially squashed.

The Great Hall of the British Museum (OPPOSITE PAGE) resembles nothing so much as the interior of a vast, formal tent ensconced in the Arabian desert; its explosive lines arcing into the sky.

LONDON

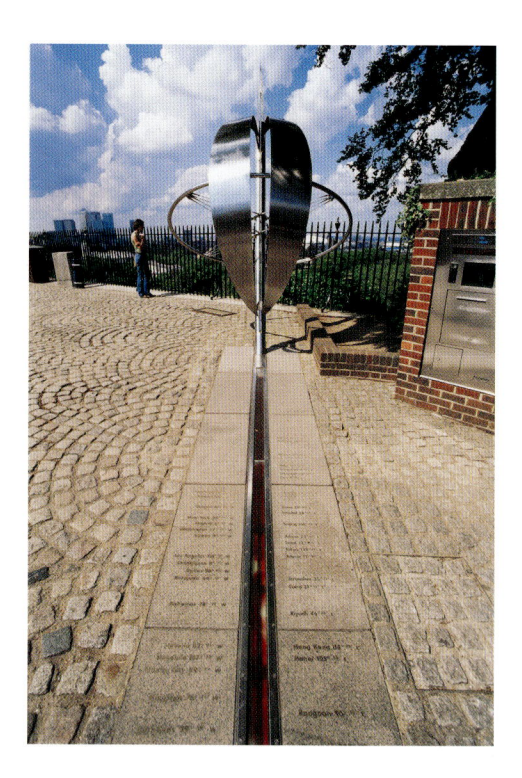

FASHIONABLE PILE: Once the largest warehouse complexes on the Thames Butler's Wharf (TOP LEFT) is now one of the most fashionable places to live in the city. Charles Dickens set Bill Sykes' den nearby in Oliver Twist.

All the world's time is set from the Greenwich Meridian (TOP RIGHT) and styled GMT or Universal Co-ordinated Time (UTC). Greenwich has attracted some VIP visitors over the centuries including Peter the Great and Bob Hope.

Looking for space to grow, the City moved east to Docklands (BOTTOM RIGHT) when the government put in place plans for the re-development of 11 of the old disused docks.

The Cutty Sark (OPPOSITE PAGE) was originally built for a life of 30 years when it was completed in 1869 racing with other tea clippers to bring the precious commodity back from India for its English aficionados.

PORTRAIT OF ENGLAND

LONDON

ROYAL FRONT DOOR: Horseguards was the original front entrance of Buckingham Palace (BELOW) and the Household Cavalry mount guard there daily.

The new guard marches out (RIGHT) from St James's Palace on its way to Buckingham Palace to replace the old guard for the Changing of the Guard. The guard is mounted by men from any one of seven regiments who do their duty alongside operational commitments.

LONDON

BOROUGH BUSINESS: There has been a market near the site of the modern Borough Market for 2,000 years (TOP LEFT).

Harrods, the ultimate department store (TOP RIGHT), is an international icon that attracts shoppers from all over the world.

If it's trinkets you're after there is only one place to go: if Portobello Market (BOTTOM RIGHT) doesn't have it then it probably doesn't exist.

From seaweed shampoo to pumice stone and lots of other things you've never heard of, Neal's Yard (OPPOSITE PAGE) offers a breathtaking array of products.

PORTRAIT OF ENGLAND

LONDON

PORTRAIT OF ENGLAND

CARIBBEAN ROOTS: For over 40 years the Notting Hill Carnival (OPPOSITE PAGE) has been putting West Indian culture on show every August.

(THIS PAGE FROM LEFT) The more outrageous the better, the London Gay Pride parade brightens up the capital every July.

Soho's Chinatown erupts every year when it's time to celebrate Chinese New Year: this young girl wears a lucky god mask.

Brother and sister proudly wear green for St Patrick's Day.

The Mela festival is a melange of music, fun and food.

LONDON

BEDS OF PLENTY: St James's Park (TOP RIGHT) is a splash of colour close to the heart of the city while Hyde Park (BOTTOM LEFT, BOTTOM RIGHT AND OPPOSITE PAGE) provides an amazing range of activities for city dwellers all year round.

PORTRAIT OF ENGLAND

LONDON

THE UNDERGROUND: One of the most recognised corporate symbols in the world (TOP LEFT) identifies the world's longest metro system. The long, underground tunnels (TOP RIGHT) give rise to the name though more than half its length is actually above ground. At Bank station (BOTTOM LEFT) the gap between platform and train is such that one visitor exclaimed: 'That's not a gap, that's a chasm.'

As in many large cities caution is the word when protecting your valuables (OPPOSITE PAGE, TOP LEFT).

The much loved Routemaster bus, (OPPOSITE PAGE, TOP RIGHT) is still in use on selected 'heritage' routes.

Heatwaves (OPPOSITE PAGE, BOTTOM RIGHT) may be rare but when they hit, the Tube is a very unpleasant place.

Stretch limousines (OPPOSITE PAGE, BOTTOM LEFT) are now so popular that sometimes the West End looks more like Chicago.

43

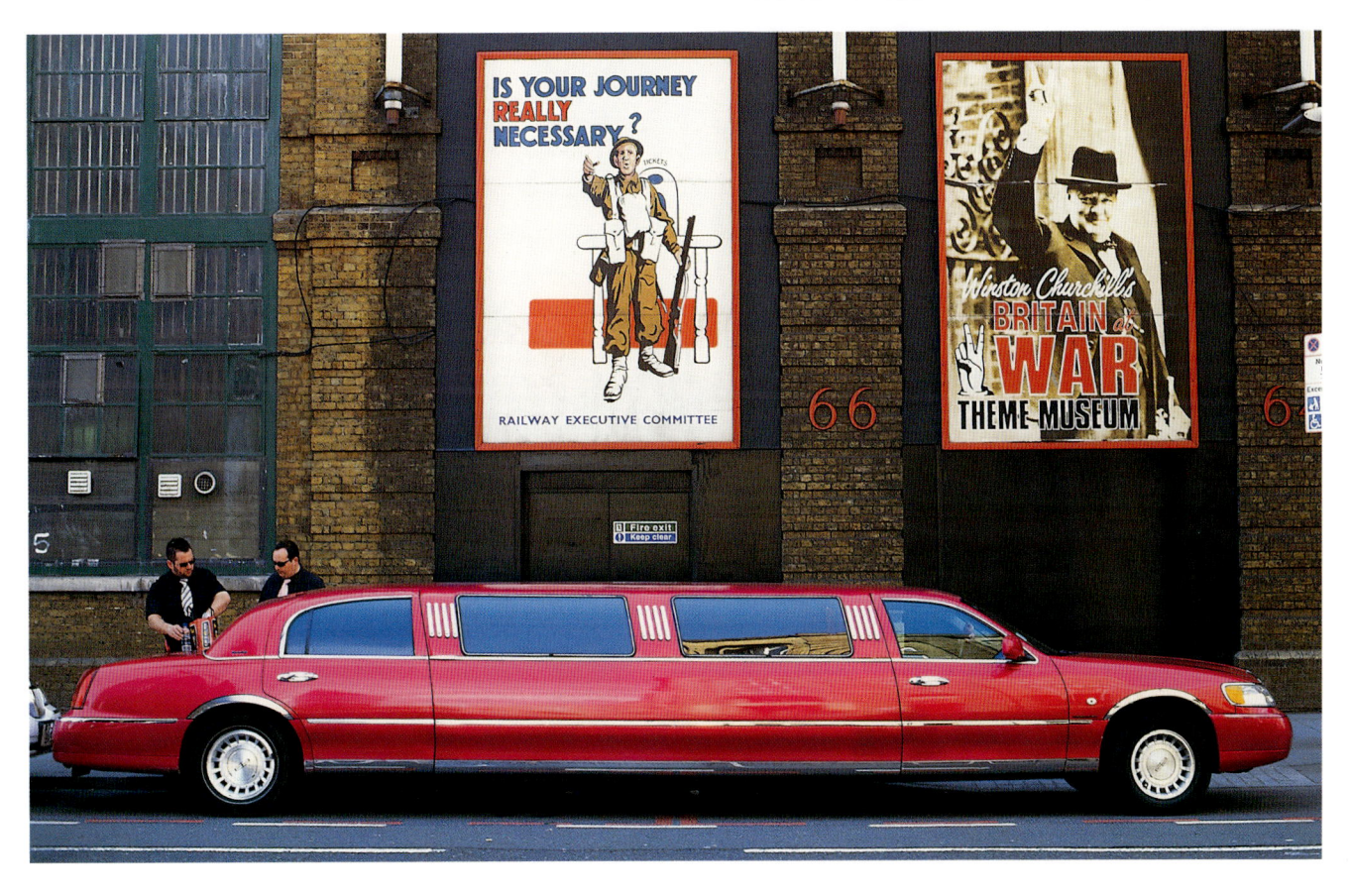

LONDON

GARDENER'S HEAVEN: Kew Gardens' (LEFT) 300 acres boast one in eight of the world's plant varieties and, as a UNESCO heritage site, is engaged in a large programme to protect the world's plant life from extinction.

Richmond borough (ABOVE) boasts 21 miles of river frontage on the Thames with choice views all the way from Hampton Court Palace to Kew Gardens.

ROYAL RETREAT: Hampton Court Palace (TOP LEFT) has provided a weekend getaway retreat for many royals and Queen Mary I spent her honeymoon relaxing in its state rooms.

This lion rampant (BOTTOM LEFT) bearing the royal coat of arms in its claws is a fine example of the many statues to be in Hampton Court's grounds.

The approaches to Hampton Court (BOTTOM RIGHT) and the famous maze are two of its many attractions.

LONDON

HOME FROM HOME: The entrance to the Queen's home outside the capital, Windsor Castle (ABOVE). The homes of few heads of state are as integrated into the surrounding society as the Queen's.

Queen Victoria (TOP RIGHT) the current Queen's most illustrious ancestor did much to shape modern Britain.

The streets of Windsor near the Castle (BOTTOM RIGHT) have a cosy, old-world air despite the constant throng of tourists.

ROYAL PROGRESS: (LEFT) The Queen makes her traditional tour of the Ascot racecourse as a part of a season some call 'the world's best party'. Queen Anne inaugurated the tradition in 1711.

The dress code at Ascot (BOTTOM LEFT) reflects an earlier, more elegant age but young women continue to try and bend the royal rules.

The Greencoats (BOTTOM RIGHT) are a body of guards charged with protecting the monarch. These days these kindly, old gentlemen are more merry than martial.

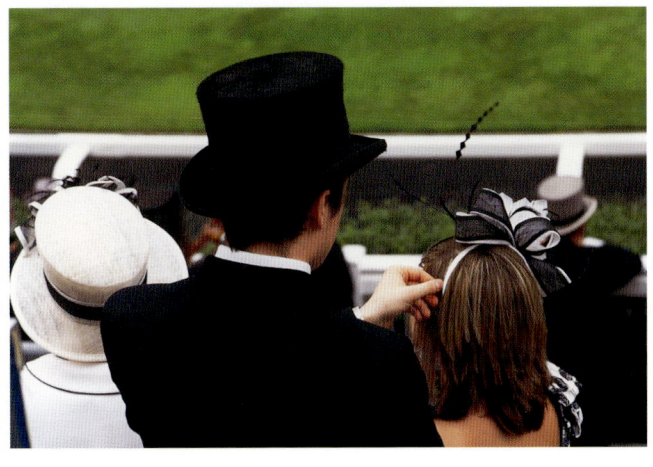

LONDON

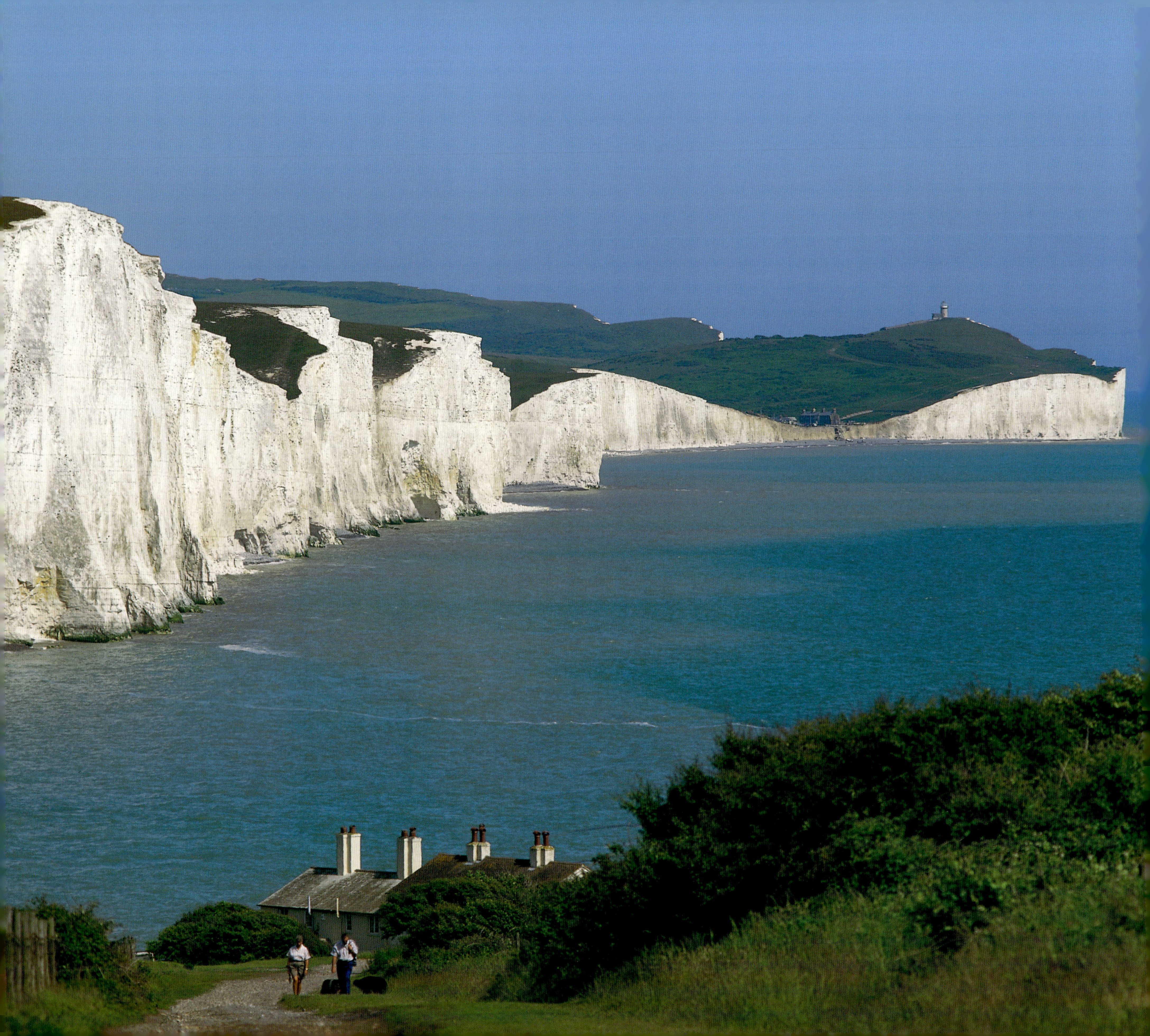

THE SOUTH

Religion, learning, military power and a soft, verdant landscape bequeath the South of England its most impressive attractions. Its great centres of learning and religion from Oxford to Canterbury mark out the southern half of the country as the equal of anywhere in Europe or the world.

Rise early and drive through England's rolling, winding lanes under pristine blue skies to get a sense of what the country's heritage is all about. The morning sun shows off the honey-coloured stone of college and cathedral. It sets off, too, the fine string of castles that have been there since time immemorial guarding against a French threat which now seems quaint but which was once very real as when French raiders laid waste to Dover.

The fine, robust and well-preserved castles of Kent stand witness to this great defensive martial tradition: Dover, Deal, Rochester and Leeds are all well worth visiting.

The rolling English road will carry you through unmatched landscapes from Hampshire to the borders of Somerset and from green orchards to lush pastures. The best place to begin your coastal tour is in Eastbourne, the relaxed seaside mood without the hustle of more fashionable and youth-oriented centres gives a sense of the elegance that once marked out its neighbour along the coast, Brighton.

Past the glory of the Seven Sisters (OPPOSITE PAGE), this seaside watering hole has all the pizzazz that comes with an almost umbilical link to London. Where it was once more of a weekend bolt-hole it is now a virtual extension of the capital's social and party scene; another satellite town even though its characteristically louche ambience far outshines its competitors.

Take in Chichester and its magnificent cathedral dating from the 11th century and its magical harbour then along the coast road to Portsmouth — home of the Royal Navy — with its great naval and maritime ambience along with HMS Victory restored in all its glory. All the navy's greatest operations have been launched from Portsmouth including the recapture of the Falkland Islands, the riskiest of a long line of naval and military adventures.

DOVER'S DEFENCE: Dover's castle (TOP RIGHT) sits four-square above the port city that stands at the closest point to the continent. The castle retained an important military role right up to the nuclear age.

Scotney Castle (BOTTOM RIGHT) has arguably the country's most romantic garden set aside this idyllic 14th century castle.

Concerts in the great bowl of green grass which makes a natural amphitheatre beside Leeds Castle (BOTTOM LEFT) are one of the truly memorable experiences of the English summer.

Rochester Castle (OPPOSITE PAGE) is one of the best-preserved Norman fortifications in spite of being under siege three times and partially demolished.

PORTRAIT OF ENGLAND

THE SOUTH

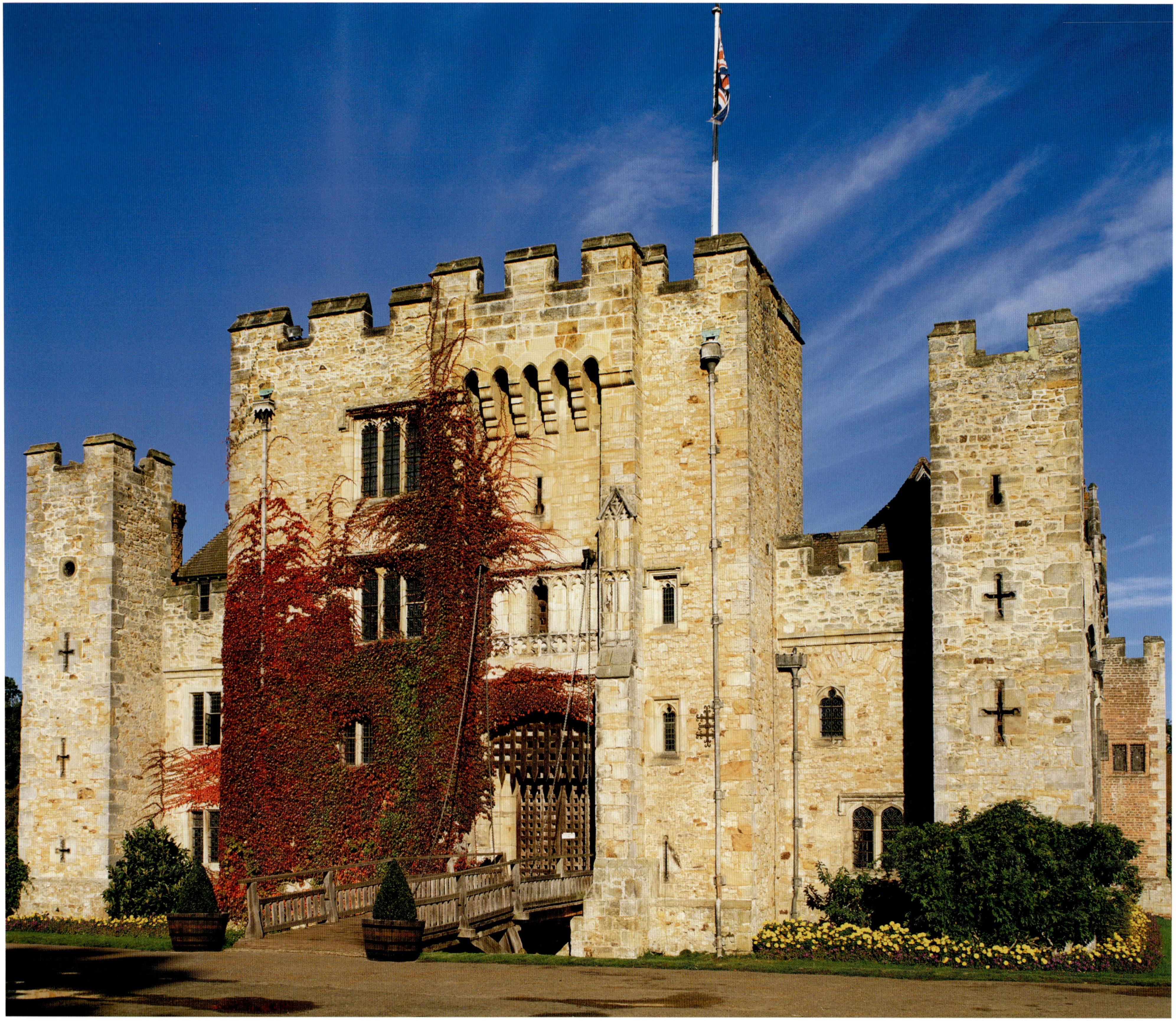

CHILDHOOD IDYLL: At least Anne Boleyn had the pleasure of childhood days at Hever Castle (OPPOSITE PAGE) before the trauma of marriage to Henry VIII.

Deal Castle (BELOW) was one of a string of new fortifications built at great speed by Henry VIII when he feared a Catholic invasion from the Continent.

Vita Sackville-West and her husband Sir Harold Nicolson created one of the world's most remarkable gardens at Sissinghurst Castle (RIGHT) after Vita bought a dilapidated Elizabethan mansion and 400 acres of farm land in 1930.

PAGAN RITES: (THIS PAGE FROM LEFT) Morris dancing is believed to have its origins in pagan times. It was later co-opted by Christianity into its present form. Morris dances mark harvests and other moments of celebration.

A Jack-in-the-Green attendant, also known as a Bogie.

The city of Rochester in Kent hosts both the colourful Sweeps Festival (THIRD FROM LEFT AND OPPOSITE PAGE) and the Dickens Festival (FOURTH FROM LEFT).

THE SOUTH

CHURCH MARTYR: Stained glass window in Canterbury Cathedral (ABOVE LEFT) and pub sign (ABOVE RIGHT) commemorate the murder of Thomas Becket in 1170. He is a saint in both Catholic and Protestant denominations because of his defence of religion against the forces of King Henry II.

Christchurch Gate (RIGHT) is the main entrance to the precinct of Canterbury Cathedral. The bronze figure of Christ above the entrance was placed there in 1991 replacing one used for target practice by Parliamentarians in 1642.

(OPPOSITE PAGE) Canterbury Cathedral is the mother church of the Anglican Communion, the world-wide Church of England.

PORTRAIT OF ENGLAND

THE SOUTH

PROSPEROUS PORT: As one of the Cinque Ports, Rye was awarded special privileges by the Crown in return for protecting the coastal region. The quality of Mermaid Street's (LEFT AND ABOVE) brick surface reflects the town's wealth. The Mermaid Inn dates back to 1420 and has accommodated many an artist of stage and screen, including Charlie Chaplin and Johnny Depp.

The town stands at the confluence of two rivers (OPPOSITE PAGE) where there is a small fishing fleet and a plethora of leisure boats.

PORTRAIT OF ENGLAND

THE SOUTH

PORTRAIT OF ENGLAND

PAPAL PENANCE: In 1070 Pope Alexander II ordered the Normans to do penance for killing so many people during their Conquest of England. William the Conqueror's response was to build Battle Abbey, the gatehouse to which still stands today (OPPOSITE PAGE).

(THIS PAGE) This fishing boat on Hastings beach is part of the largest beach-based fleet in the country. Fresh seafood and traditional fish and chips attract day-trippers and seagulls alike.

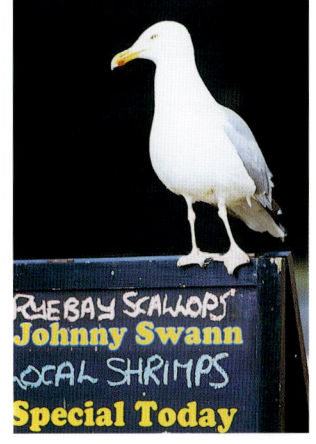

THE SOUTH

PORTRAIT OF ENGLAND

COASTAL WALK: The sight of the Seven Sisters is one of the most striking views on the exciting five-mile beach walk from Birling Gap to Cuckmere Haven on the Sussex coast.

THE SOUTH

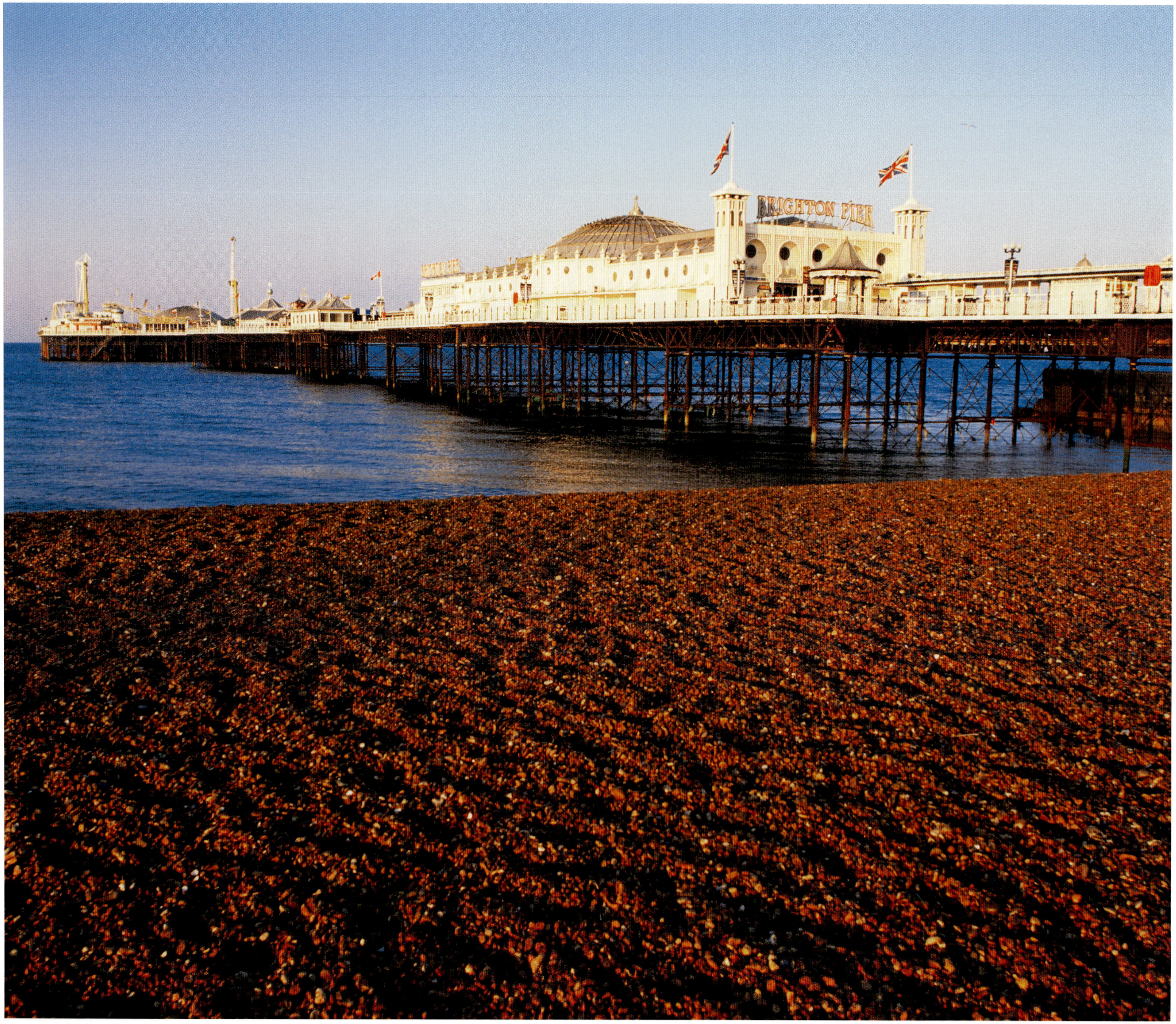
BRIGHTON PIER

PIER PLEASURE: Built in 1899 Brighton pier (opposite page) is a classic late Victorian example with arcades and amusements stretching out over the surf.

When the Prince of Wales wanted to carry on a secret liaison with his mistress, Brighton was the setting for their canoodling. As King George IV, he decided he wanted something a little more grand and commissioned the Royal Pavilion (top and bottom left).

Seaside fun fairs are summer attractions along the whole length of the south coast and Brighton, the first truly fashionable summer resort, is no exception (bottom right).

THE SOUTH

SUNNY WORTHING: This idyllic spot between Brighton and Bognor Regis lives up to its 1890s advertising slogan and nickname and the small boats drawn up on the beach suggests its easy-going atmosphere.

A SPIRE TO BE VIEWED: Modern Chichester has no trace of its attractions as a landfall for the invading Romans apart from the proximity of the ocean. Today it is known for its annual July arts festival and glorious cathedral, the only one in England visible from the sea.

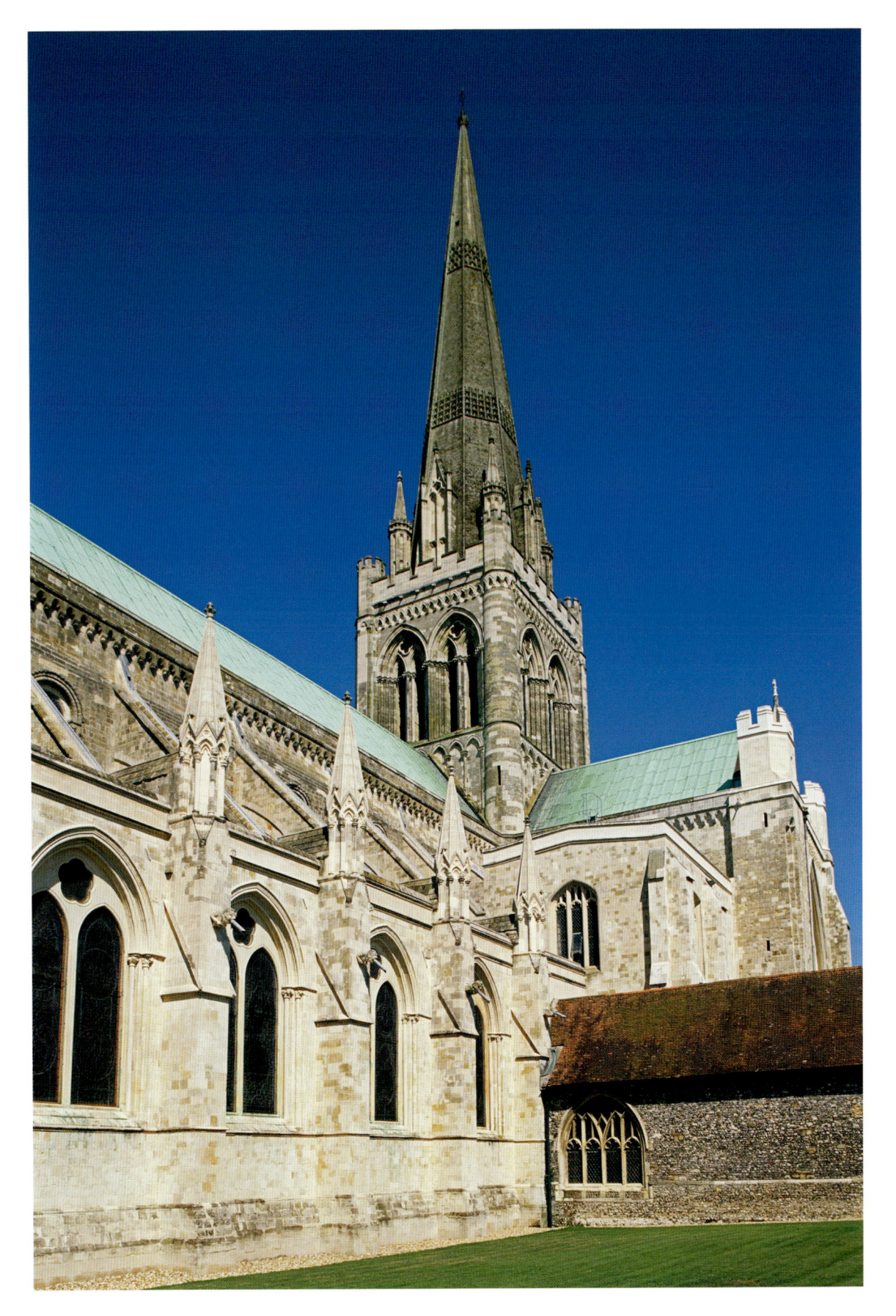

THE SOUTH

NELSON'S PRIDE: HMS Victory looks as impressive today in Portsmouth as when she bore Admiral Nelson to victory over combined French and Spanish fleets at the Battle of Trafalgar in 1805.

GEORGIAN GEMS: The Georgian architecture alone makes Alresford in Hampshire (TOP LEFT AND BOTTOM RIGHT) worth a visit.

This couple (BOTTOM LEFT) get into the spirit of things in Georgian dress at the Pantiles, Tunbridge Wells.

THE SOUTH

WINCHESTER WONDER: Winchester Cathedral has had the distinction of having the longest aisle in Europe since it was built in 1079. The city has been voted as the best place to live in the United Kingdom.

PORTRAIT OF ENGLAND

SALISBURY SPLENDOUR: The cathedral that inspired Handel to write several of his works during his time in England. It boasts the tallest spire in the country at 404 feet.

PORTRAIT OF ENGLAND

IDYLLIC ISLE: The Needles (OPPOSITE PAGE) exemplify the Isle of Wight and its great tradition of sport sailing during Cowes Week.

A family soaks up the sun and fends off the breeze on Sandown Beach (BOTTOM LEFT).

An inviting pub (TOP RIGHT) near Shanklin combines the best of village and seaside life.

Alum beach (BOTTOM RIGHT) is beautiful as well as historic: Marconi made his first radio broadcast from nearby.

JURASSIC PLAYGROUND: Looking like a dinosaur taking a morning drink from the sea, Durdle Door is an arch of limestone (ABOVE).

Man o' War beach (RIGHT) which arcs round from Durdle Door is one of the most popular beaches on Dorset's Jurassic coast near Lulworth.

THE SOUTH

PORTRAIT OF ENGLAND

GOLDEN HARVEST: A field of rape (OPPOSITE PAGE) typifies the new trend in farming which rewards growth of the crop for animal feed stock and green fuels.

Rape is cutting into pastures which are vital for dairy herds (LEFT) while the presence of a young lamb (BOTTOM RIGHT) and cock pheasant (BOTTOM LEFT) testify to the health of the countryside.

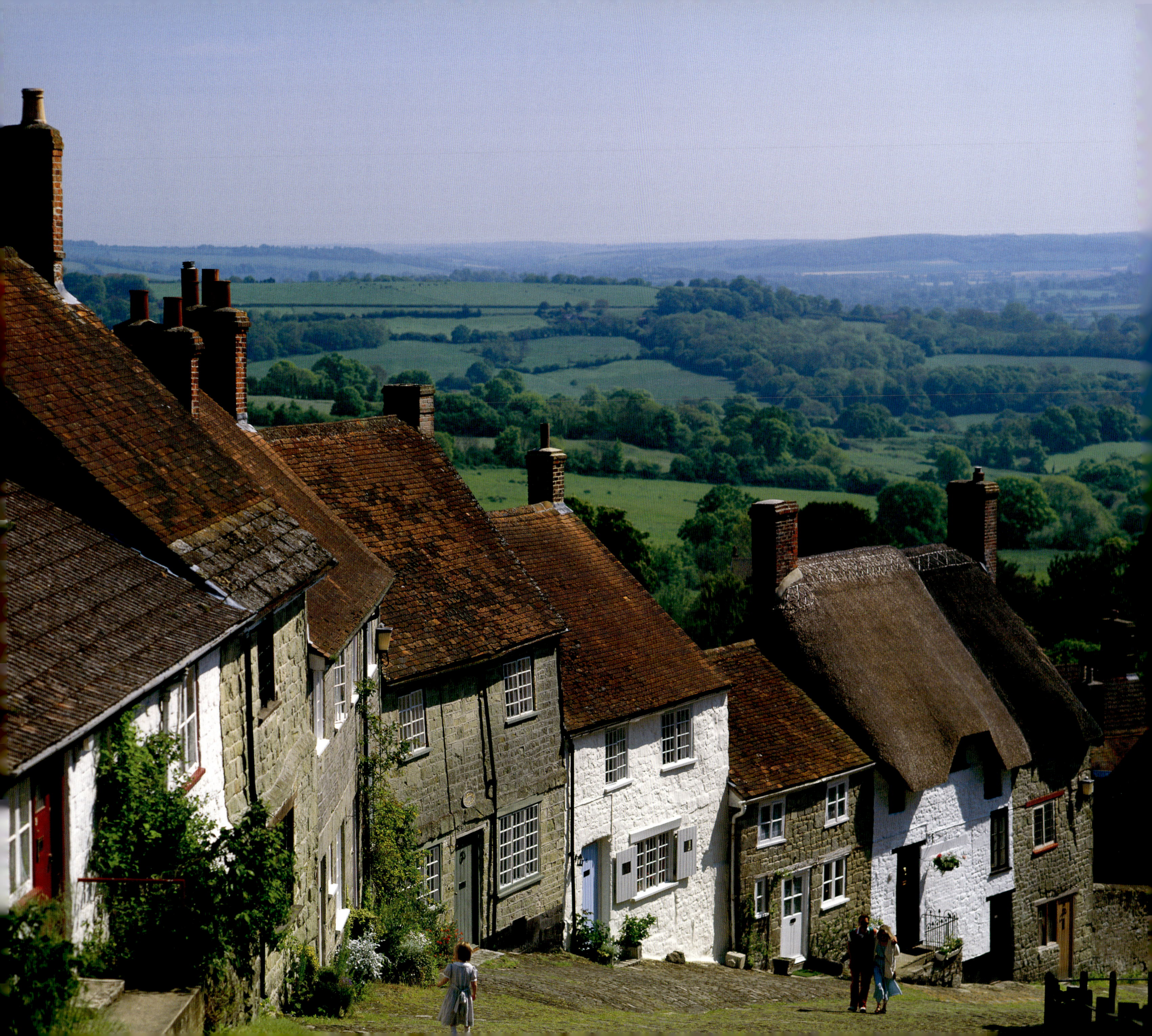

THE SOUTH WEST

The west is an area of lush river valleys, windy downland and stretches of wild, untamed moorland. It is known for its rich Cheddar cheeses and wool which used to be exported to Europe or dispatched to the ancient mill towns.

Interspersed in this varied landscape are quaint and picturesque towns like Shaftesbury (OPPOSITE PAGE) with its 18th century cottages lining Gold Hill or majestic cities like Bath and Salisbury.

The folk of the West country have always been consciously different from the rest of the country with little time for the establishment of the south-east around London or the industrial Midlands to the north.

It is a land of mystery and imagination from which sprang the legendary King Arthur and his Knights of the Round Table who is thought to have led the English resistance to the Saxon invasion in the 6th century.

Today tourists and young people in search of adventure come to a place where they hope some of the creative energy and sense of freedom will rub off on them.

The annual Glastonbury Festival sees modern music played in an ancient landscape and leaves memories and experiences which will last a lifetime. Lulworth Cove, Durdle Door, the resorts of Bournemouth, Weymouth and Weston-Super-Mare are seaside attractions unrivalled anywhere else in the country. Stonehenge and the stone circle at Avebury are even more remarkable.

For families Devon and Cornwall abound in excellent beaches from Porthleven to St Ives Bay, Perranporth and Newquay while seaborne activities are as many and varied as anywhere in the country.

MONASTIC WEALTH: Glastonbury Abbey was one of the wealthiest monasteries in the country (TOP RIGHT AND BOTTOM LEFT). Today the remains of this fine building cover 36 acres.

Shopping in the local high street (BOTTOM RIGHT) brings a feast of alternative options reminiscent of the Far East during the days of the hippie trail.

Glastonbury Tor at dawn (OPPOSITE PAGE) is no ordinary hill. It's said to be the home of Gwyn ap Nudd, the king of the fairies and visitors who enjoy the view from the top claim they are transformed.

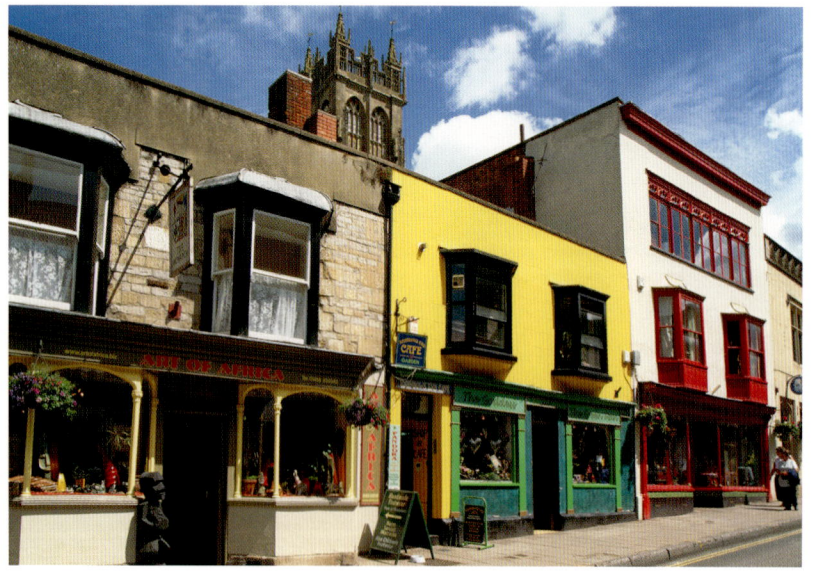

THE SOUTH WEST

DAWN MIST: A thin veil of mist rises from the lush, flat plain that stretches out beneath Glastonbury Tor.

THE SOUTH WEST

PORTRAIT OF ENGLAND

STONEHENGE DRAMA: The ancient stones appear out of the dawn mist adding to the air of mystery that surrounds a structure that dates from about 2,500 BC (OPPOSITE PAGE).

Avebury stone circle (LEFT AND BELOW) predates Stonehenge by some 500 years though the stones are smaller and the setting less dramatic than its more famous neighbour.

THE SOUTH WEST

PORTRAIT OF ENGLAND

MAJESTIC BATH: Royal Crescent (OPPOSITE PAGE) is the city's foremost example of Palladian architecture which is arguably the finest street in England.

A barge cruises along the River Avon which encircles the main body of the city (ABOVE).

Bath's Roman heritage, which was the key to its success as a spa town, is evident in the baths (RIGHT).

THE SOUTH WEST

CHEDDAR GORGE (BELOW): The dramatic chasm, which is up to 400 feet deep, has caves which were once used to store the famous cheese of the same name because of the high humidity and the constant temperature.

Magnificent Wells Cathedral (OPPOSITE PAGE) contains 300 medieval statues of kings, knights and saints, many of them life size, on its west front alone.

THE SOUTH WEST

PORTRAIT OF ENGLAND

POLPERRO PARADISE: The picture-book port nestled in a tiny, peaceful cove in Cornwall is composed of fishermen's cottages — 'ships in stone' — giving no hint that it was once a centre for the smuggling of brandy and tobacco.

PORTRAIT OF ENGLAND

ENGLISH RIVIERA: Babbacombe Bay near Torquay is one of Devon's most popular bathing beaches (OPPOSITE PAGE).

Brixham is Torquay's fishing port neighbour and its neat harbour contains a replica of Sir Francis Drake's ship the Golden Hind (BELOW).

RELIGIOUS EXPERIENCE: Legend has it that St Michael appeared at St Michael's Mount in 495 AD. When the Normans conquered England they were struck by the similarity with Mont St Michel in France and invited Benedictine monks to build a small monastery.

THE SOUTH WEST

FUTURE PERFECT: The Eden Project is a perfect example of recycling an old industrial site: in this case a disused clay pit that now houses a global garden for the 21st century.

WORLD'S END: Land's End is the westerly-most point of the country but the most southerly, Lizard Point, is a few miles south-east.

PICTURE PERFECT: Appropriately for an artists' colony, St Ives enjoys some dramatic Atlantic sunrises and sunsets (LEFT).

The harbour is home to a varied fleet of small leisure boats (BELOW) while the Tate West gallery has enhanced the town's reputation as a centre of culture.

BEACH EXTRAVAGANZA: Newquay's splendid beaches illustrate why the resort is so popular. Towan Beach is popular with bathers (ABOVE) while Fistral Beach (RIGHT) is a must for any surfing enthusiast.

LEGENDARY LAND: Tintagel Castle ruin is inextricably linked with the stories of King Arthur and his Knights of the Round Table.

PRIVATE INVESTMENT: Clovelly in Devon (TOP AND BOTTOM RIGHT) has been a noted regional beauty spot ever since it starred in the novel of the Spanish Armada, 'Westward Ho!' The village is privately owned and its cobbled streets rise steeply from the harbour.

The largest seaside resort in North Devon, Ilfracombe (BOTTOM LEFT) nestles in the elbow of a bay and divides itself into two communities, the farming fraternity around the parish church and the fishermen around the port.

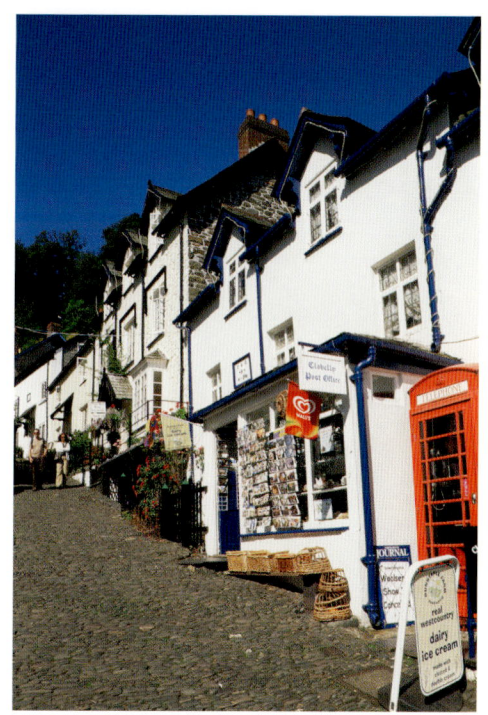

THE SOUTH WEST

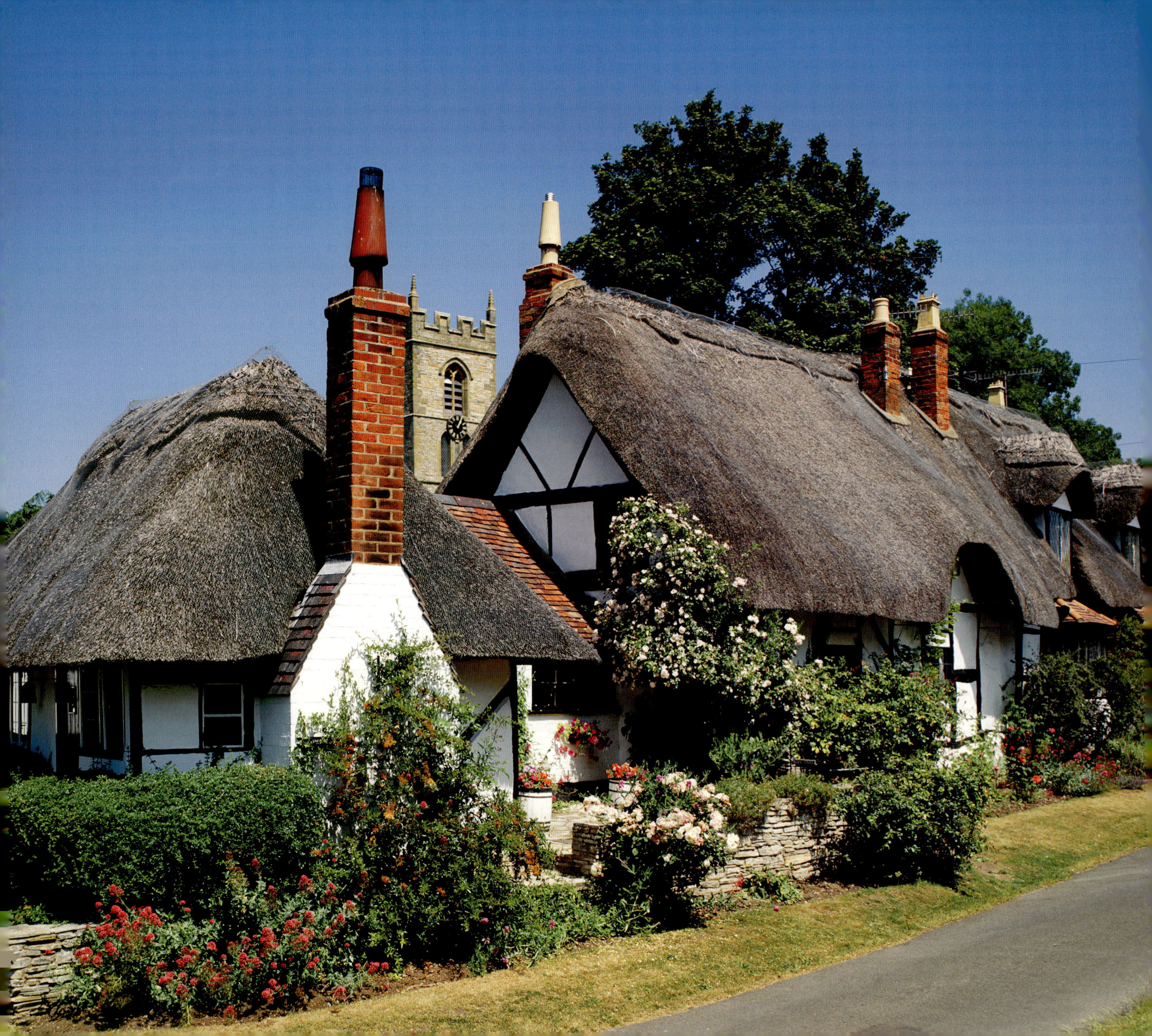

CENTRAL ENGLAND

The Midlands conjures up images of heavy industry, brick kilns and smoking chimneys but there is much more than that to central England. Ranging from glorious Gloucester in the south to Birmingham and the potteries of Stoke on Trent in the north the region has a greater range of interest for the visitor than practically any other.

The neat, model villages of the Cotswolds such as Welford-upon-Avon (OPPOSITE PAGE) with their broad greens, honey-coloured stone, thatched roofs and local produce reflect a by-gone age which has fascination for current generations. To the north-east is the whole rich heritage of literature and architecture surrounding William Shakespeare and his birthplace at Stratford-upon-Avon. Before moving into the industrial heartland that is Birmingham, Coventry's role as a centre of car manufacture may have declined but its remarkable cathedral must be witnessed.

The role of industry in the history of England and its role in wealth generation is well described in regional museums such as those at Ironbridge Gorge where, in 1709, the use of inexpensive coke rather than charcoal was pioneered to produce steel powering what came to be known as the industrial revolution. The original ironbridge stills spans the river Severn. The extraordinary 2,000 miles of the canal system which are still navigable, thanks to local enthusiasts and the tourist industry, retell a fascinating story for those with the time to take their travel more slowly.

The black and white timber-framed houses that abound in the area illustrate the wealth the region created and the desire to display it through such buildings as Little Moreton Hall, 10 miles north of Stoke-on-Trent or the dazzling Burghley House in Leicestershire.

BROADWAY MELODY: The town was once an important coach-stop on the route between Leicester and London and that heritage created one of the finest hotels in England, the Lygon Arms (BOTTOM RIGHT).

Art Galleries and boutiques line either side of the 'Broad Way' one of the longest high streets in England (TOP LEFT).

The Broadway Tower (TOP RIGHT), a folly built by the Earl of Coventry, is the highest point in the Cotswolds.

Cotswold countryside (OPPOSITE PAGE) is rolling, rich, colourful and a magnet for city-dwellers determined on a weekend cottage or something for retirement.

CENTRAL ENGLAND

PORTRAIT OF ENGLAND

COTSWOLD CALM: The village of Upper Slaughter (OPPOSITE PAGE) is almost entirely untouched by modern commercialism and can best be reached on foot. The name has nothing to do with blood-letting but is rooted in the old English for muddy place.

Bourton-On-The-Water (TOP LEFT) and Burford (BELOW) are centres for tourists visiting the Cotswolds and boast a fine range of shops, galleries and restaurants. Both are conscious of their exotically named neighbours and roots in agriculture (CENTRE AND BOTTOM LEFT).

CENTRAL ENGLAND

MOTHER'S PRIDE: The home of William Shakespeare's mother Mary Arden (TOP LEFT) is in the village of Wilmcote outside Stratford-upon-Avon. Anne Hathaway's cottage (OPPOSITE PAGE) and the Shakespeare statue and Shakespeare Centre (TOP AND BOTTOM RIGHT) are both in the Bard's birthplace.

PORTRAIT OF ENGLAND

CENTRAL ENGLAND

PORTRAIT OF ENGLAND

FRIENDS IN NEED: The almshouses of the Lord Leycester Hospital in Warwick (TOP LEFT) are for the families of retired servicemen.

Warwick Castle (OPPOSITE PAGE AND TOP AND BOTTOM RIGHT) is one of the finest and most complete medieval fortresses in the country. The great hall and state rooms display a collection of family treasures from around the world while mounted knights in the castle's colours can be seen in action.

PORTRAIT OF ENGLAND

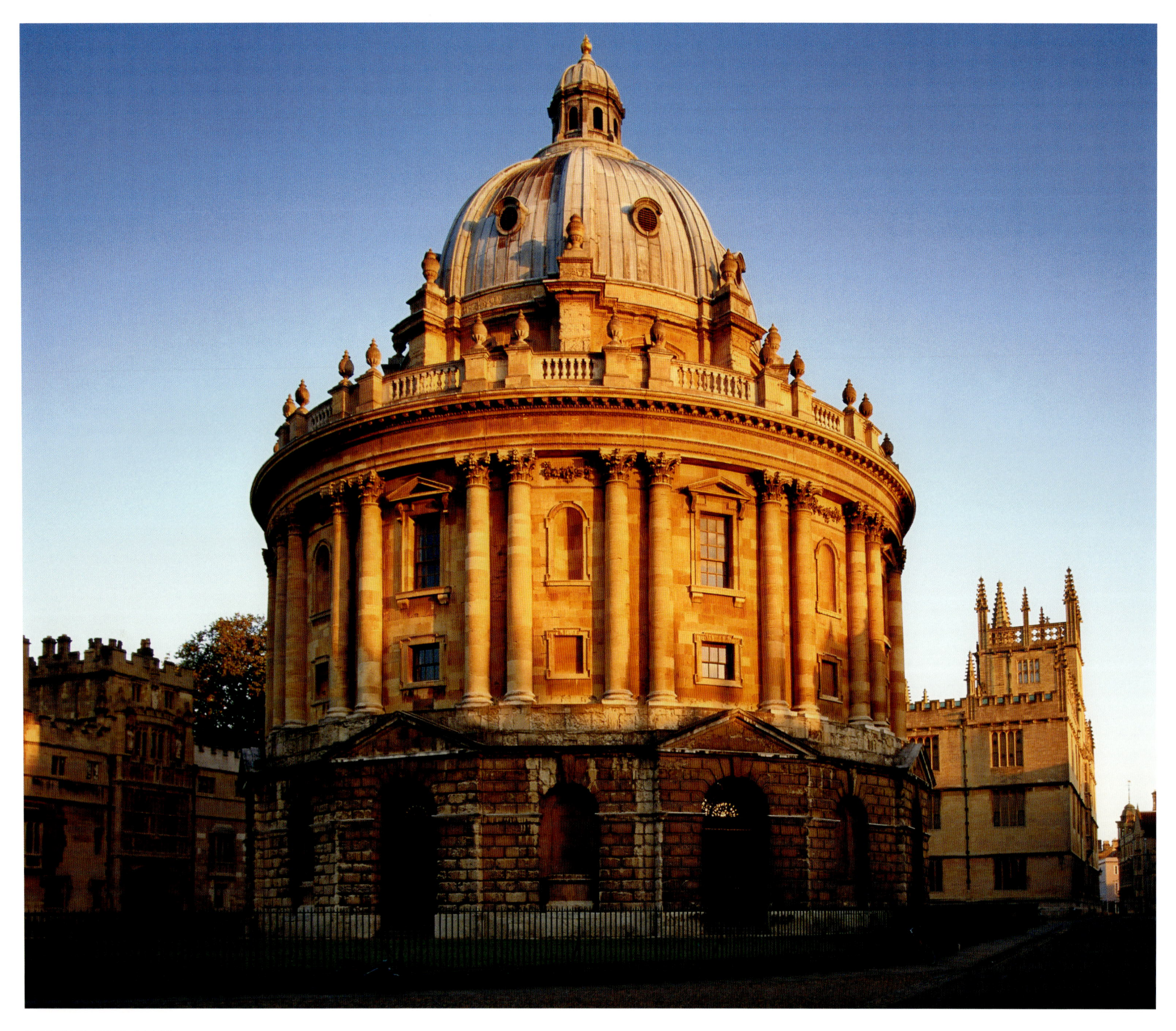

MEDICAL MEMORIAL: The striking domed baroque rotunda, the Radcliffe Camera in Oxford, was built as a tribute to the physician Dr John Radcliffe (OPPOSITE PAGE).

The city's breathtaking architecture is evident in the Bridge of Sighs at Hertford College (ABOVE); the doorway to All Souls College (TOP RIGHT) and the Christ Church of St Mary the Virgin in High Street (BOTTOM RIGHT).

CENTRAL ENGLAND

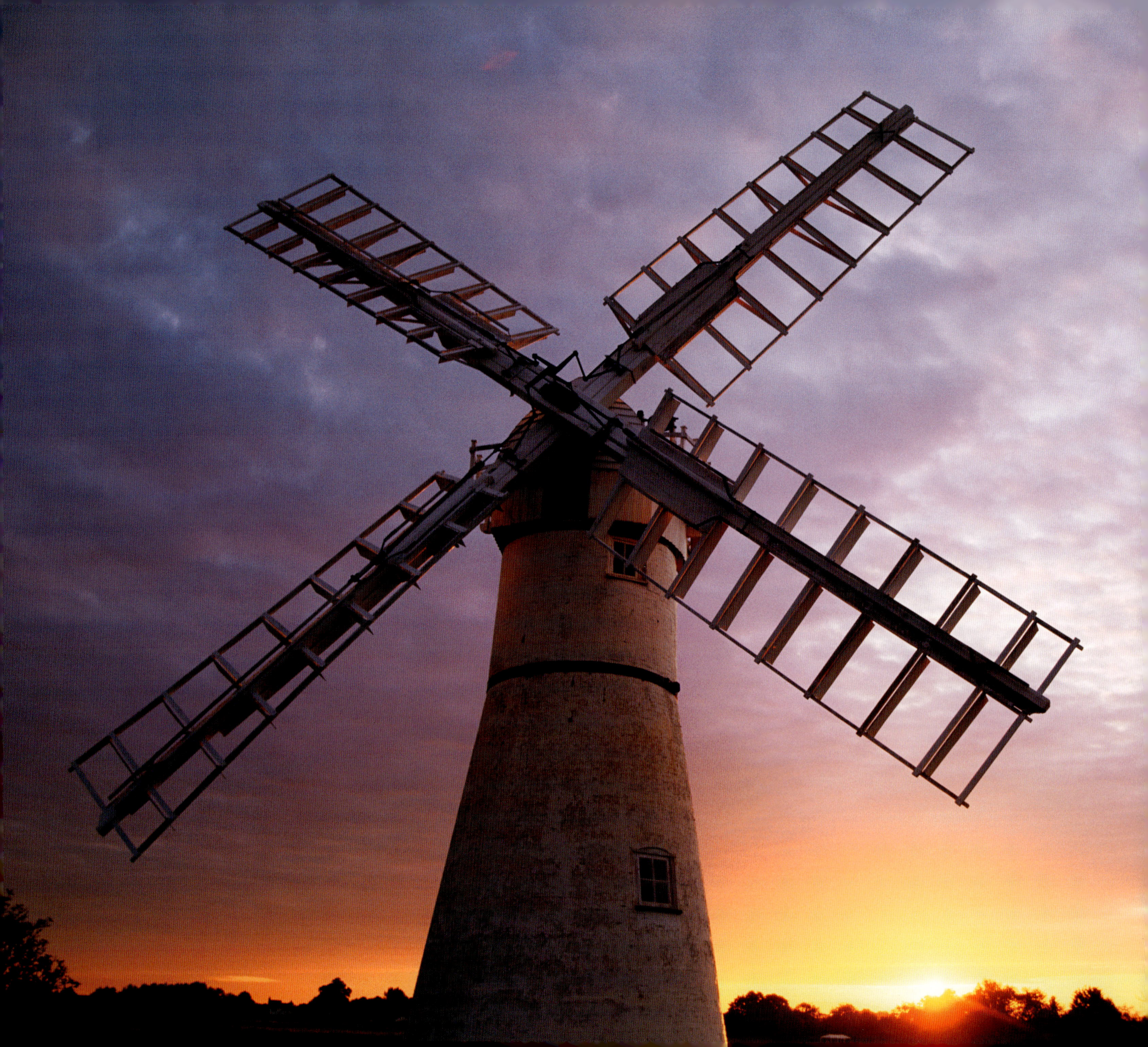

EASTERN ENGLAND

Eastern England tends to get overlooked with the major visitor focus on London and the south-east of England but it offers some of the finest recreation areas in the country and has some of the longest hours of sunshine and highest average temperatures. Though the area is flat it is not featureless and its people have great independence of thought and opinion: among the region's sons and daughters are Tom Paine, the revolutionary writer who authored The Rights of Man; Queen Boadicea who resisted the Roman invasion and whose followers burned down London, St Albans and Colchester in the process and Cromwell, creator of England's short-lived republic.

The most pleasant route into East Anglia threads its way through Constable country via John Constable's favourite locations in Dedham, East Bergholt and Flatford Mill. Diversions into Colchester, the oldest recorded town in Britain and the effective capital at the time of the Roman invasion in 43 AD, and Cambridge for the wonders of the university colleges' architecture are well advised but East Anglia's unique appeal is in its water-born sports on the Broads. Thought at first to be a natural phenomenon these stretches of water were actually created when medieval peat diggings were flooded in the 13th century. During the summer they offer 125 miles of navigable waterways unhindered by locks but teeming with enthusiasts who either like to sail in the traditional manner or prefer motor power. Strategically placed pubs and restaurants ensure that this is a part of the country where you will want to spend a lot of time. Thurne Mill, by the village of the same name, (OPPOSITE PAGE) is one of the picturesque sights along the way.

The northern Norfolk coastal area — taking in a journey from Hunstanton round to Cromer — will reveal some of the county's most beautiful countryside, including the magnificent Holkham Hall, and the bizarre effects of silting which have left ports which were once on the sea front far inland.

But no visit to the area would be complete without the place that is often considered England's most perfect small town, Lavenham. Built on the wealth generated by the wool trade its timber-framed houses are a delight.

BROADS WELCOME: The Swan at Horning (BELOW) has its origins in a cottage dating from 1696 and is popular with sailors and hikers alike.

The sails of Horsey Mill (RIGHT) used to be stopped in the shape of St Andrew's cross to warn smugglers if customs men were approaching.

(OPPOSITE PAGE, TOP LEFT) Sailors cruise past a mill on the River Thurne. (OPPOSITE PAGE, TOP RIGHT) A sign for one of the quieter parts of the Broads, the village of Martham. (OPPOSITE PAGE, BOTTOM RIGHT) Perhaps the most picturesque stretch of water on the Broads, the River Ant.

EASTERN ENGLAND

PORTRAIT OF ENGLAND

PASTEL PERFECTION: The timbered buildings of Lavenham (OPPOSITE PAGE, ABOVE AND RIGHT), decorated in a wide range of pastel tints, are so highly valued that 300 of them are protected. In medieval times its wool trade made it one of the 20 wealthiest towns in the country.

EASTERN ENGLAND

THE GREATS: The Great Gate of Trinity College (BOTTOM LEFT) exemplifies the rich architectural heritage of Cambridge which includes Trinity College (TOP RIGHT); King's College Chapel (BOTTOM RIGHT) and the entrance to King's College (BOTTOM CENTRE).

(OPPOSITE PAGE) A ubiquitous Cambridge cyclist passes the Gothic façade of King's College.

PORTRAIT OF ENGLAND

EASTERN ENGLAND

THE CLASSICS: The Great Court of Trinity College (BOTTOM LEFT); St John's College (TOP RIGHT) and the entrance to the college (BOTTOM RIGHT).

(OPPOSITE PAGE) Punting on the River Cam with St John's College and the Bridge of Sighs in the background.

PORTRAIT OF ENGLAND

EASTERN ENGLAND

BEACH BEAUTIES: Three hundred beach huts are strung along the beach at Southwold in Suffolk in a colourful necklace, contributing to the pre-war atmosphere in this fashionable resort.

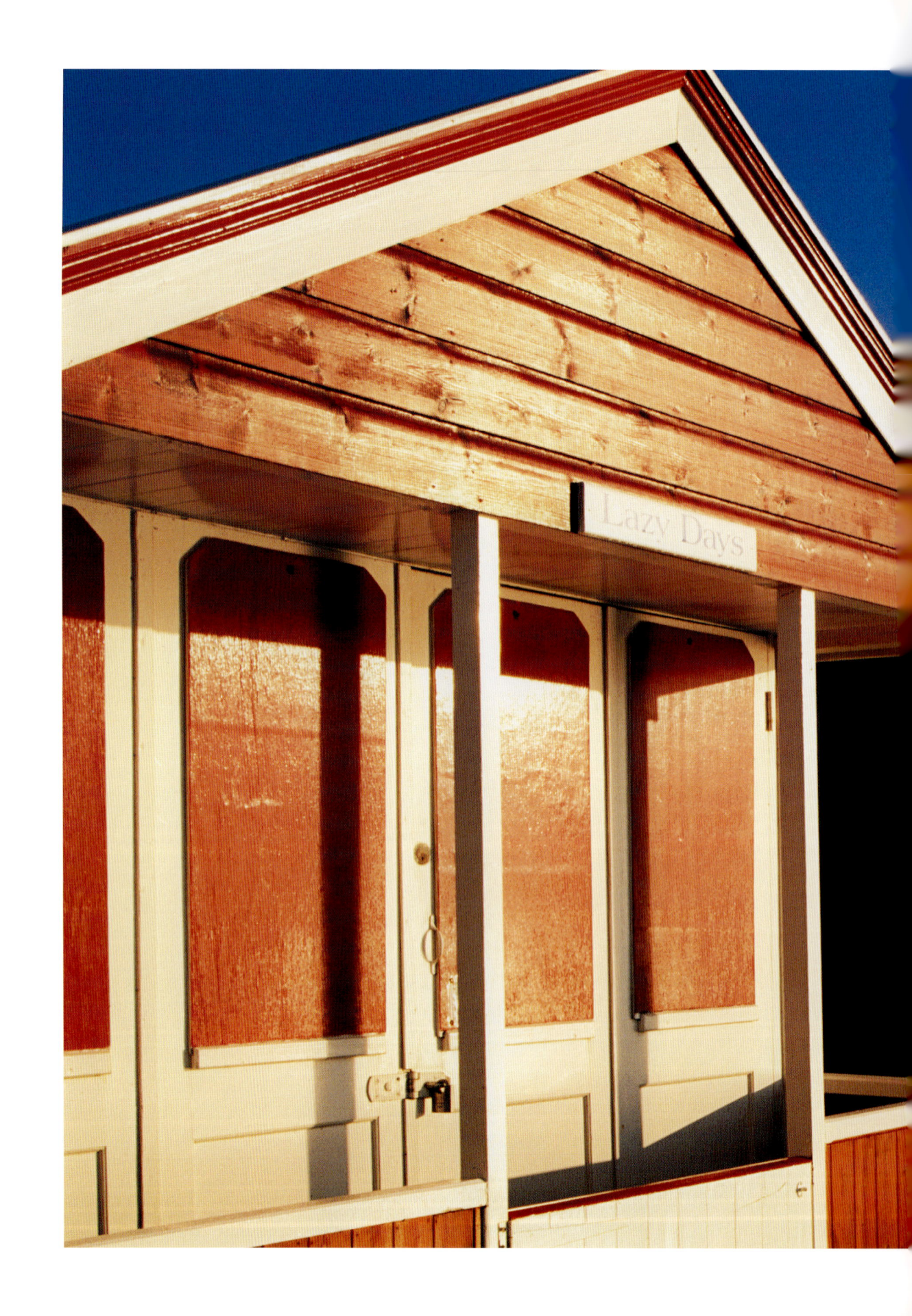

EASTERN ENGLAND

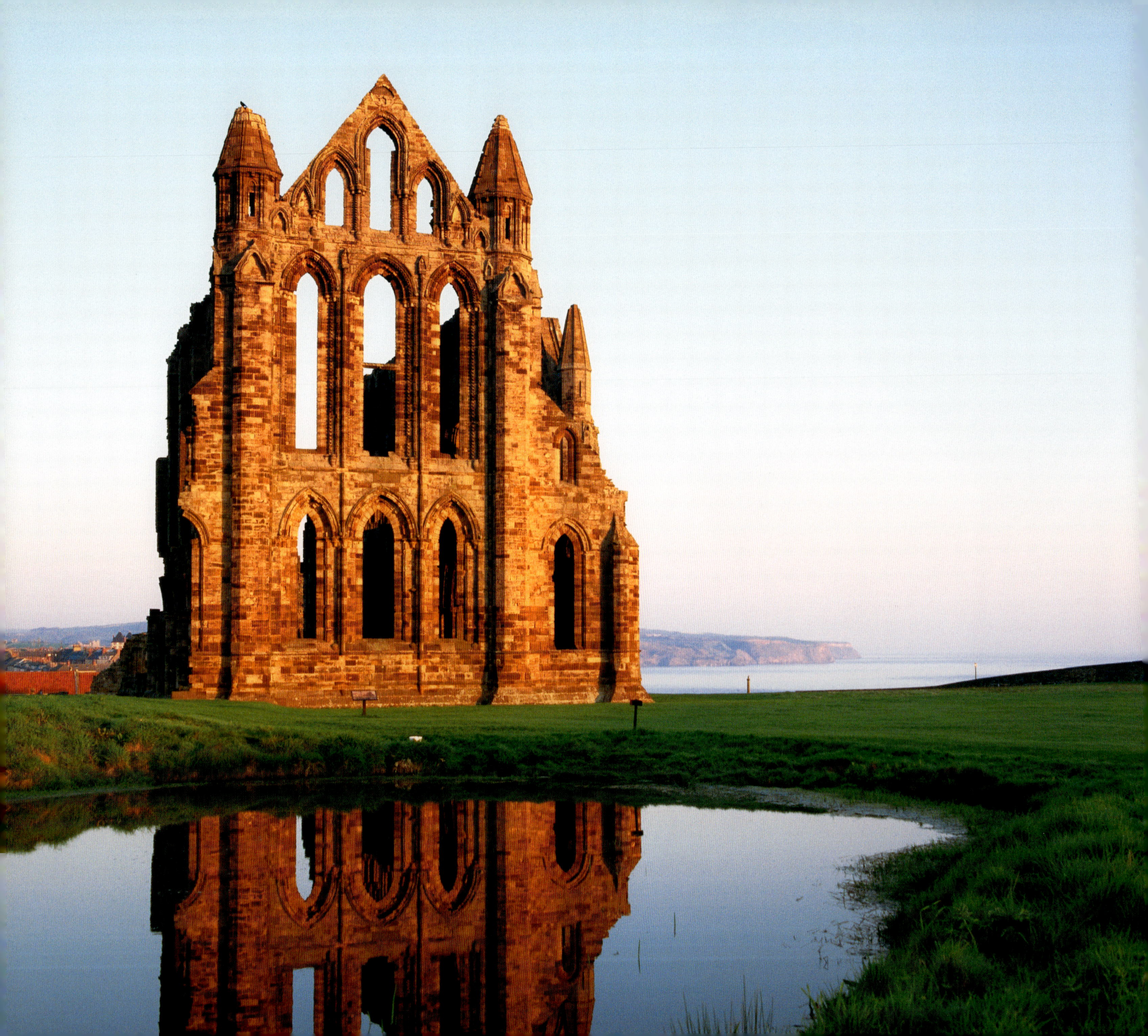

THE NORTH

In the great north-south debate the north always feels that it gets the worst of the bargain: even the weather seems to be better in the south. The north's contributions to the country, both ancient and modern, are inestimable. Some of the first influences of Christianity came through the north, a broad spectrum of its racial and cultural influences were transmitted from the continent through the north and in terms of invention and industry it has had an indelible role in the making of modern England.

The great coal mines of the north fuelled the industrial geniuses that brought the invention of the steam engine and the heavy industry and shipbuilding on the rivers Tees and Tyne, yards that built the fleet that founded and developed the empire and took the military to battle in two world-wide wars. Today the area is a centre for high-efficiency modern plants such as Nissan at Sunderland and a clutch of high-tech manufacturers which compliment the region's agricultural output.

Despite the feeling that the area is somehow disadvantaged compared with the south, the reality is that quality of life and purchasing power often more than make up the difference. Newcastle-upon-Tyne has one of Europe's largest and most modern shopping centres and, along with Gateshead, it features a range of exciting and innovative architecture. And with natural beauty from the coast of Northumbria and Lindisfarne, or Holy Island, to the Yorkshire Dales within striking distance the region has much to offer. The Lake District's tranquil beauty offers something for everyone: hill walking and hiking, boating or merely relaxing by any of the 20 major lakes and innumerable small tarns in the area.

The North Sea coast from the Scottish border at Berwick on Tweed all the way south to Whitby in North Yorkshire offers nuggets of beauty, neat ports and history aplenty since Captain James Cook served his apprenticeship there. A statue above Whitby harbour commemorates his discoveries standing not far from the ruins of the 13th century abbey (OPPOSITE PAGE). The broad acres of the Vale of York lead on to some of the cultural gems such as Rievaulx and Fountains Abbeys and the great country houses of Newby Hall, Castle Howard and Harewood House and the masterpiece itself, the city of York.

PORTRAIT OF ENGLAND

LINCOLN'S GLORY: The Victorian writer John Ruskin said that the Gothic Lincoln Cathedral (opposite page) was worth two of any other English churches.

The aptly named Steep Hill in Lincoln (above and right) is flanked with historical buildings dating back to the 12th century.

VICTORIAN ELEGANCE: Chester's Eastgate clock (TOP LEFT) built to mark Queen Victoria's Diamond Jubilee in 1897, is said to be the most photographed clock in England after Big Ben in London.

Despite their medieval appearance, many of Chester's unique 'rows' or galleries date from the Victorian era (ABOVE).

Julie Mitchell, the town crier, (BOTTOM LEFT) was the world's leading woman crier in the 1999 championships held in Vancouver.

ENGLISH ICON: This statue of Robin Hood (BELOW) in Nottingham helps keep alive a story that still has magical power today.

The Iron Bridge in Shropshire (RIGHT) is the world's first iron arch bridge, erected in 1779.

THE NORTH

PORTRAIT OF ENGLAND

PEAK PARK: The Peak District National Park in Derbyshire (OPPOSITE PAGE) was the country's first when it was established in 1951. The park contains almost 3,000 listed buildings.

Chatsworth House near Bakewell in Derbyshire (BELOW) is the home of the Duke and Duchess of Devonshire and has regular cutting-edge exhibitions of art and sculpture.

MIGHTY MINSTER: York Minster (BELOW LEFT AND OPPOSITE PAGE) is the second largest Gothic cathedral in Northern Europe whose interior (BELOW RIGHT) is equally impressive.

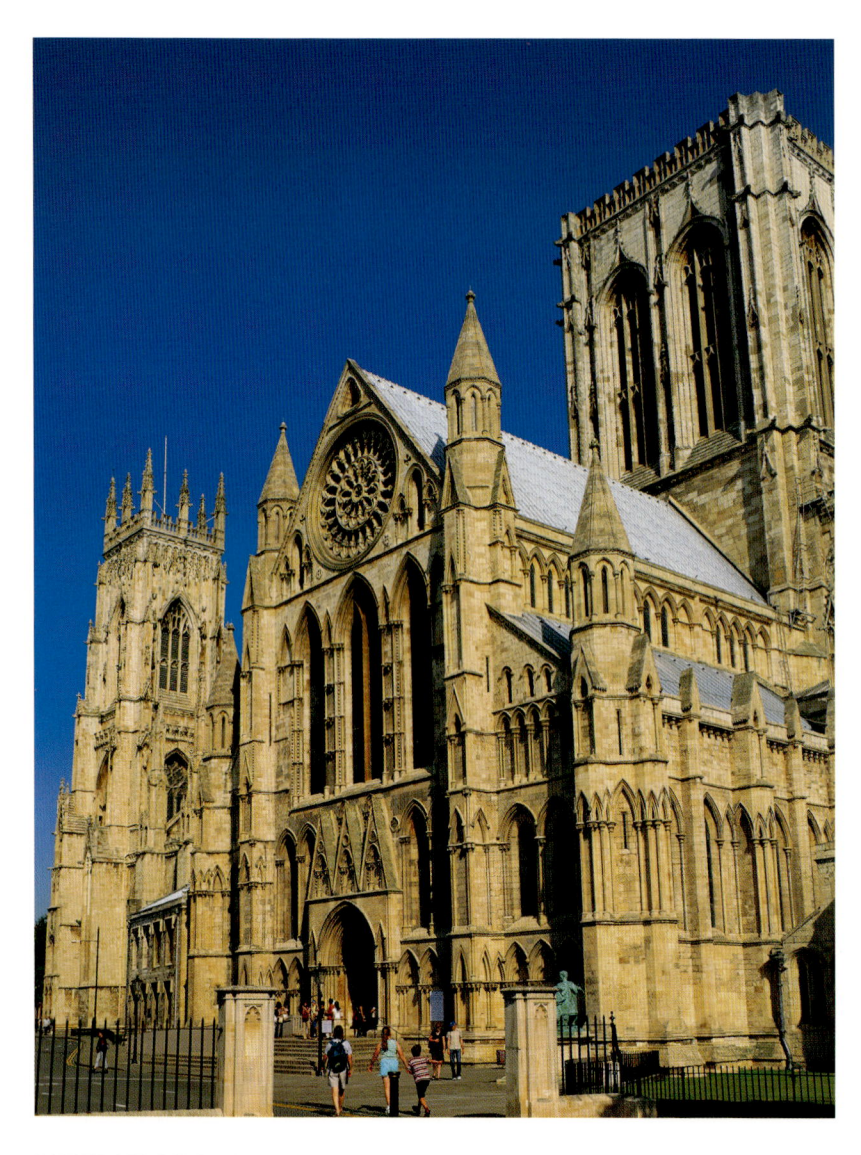

THE NORTH

PRIME PRESERVATION: The Shambles in York (BOTTOM LEFT AND TOP RIGHT) is the best-preserved medieval street in Europe where the 15th century buildings almost touch in the middle of the passageway.

(BOTTOM RIGHT) The scourge of parliament, Guy Fawkes, who almost succeeded in blowing it up, was born in York in 1570.

Clifford's Tower, (OPPOSITE PAGE) the last remaining fragment of York Castle, got its name when Roger de Clifford was executed for treason there in 1322.

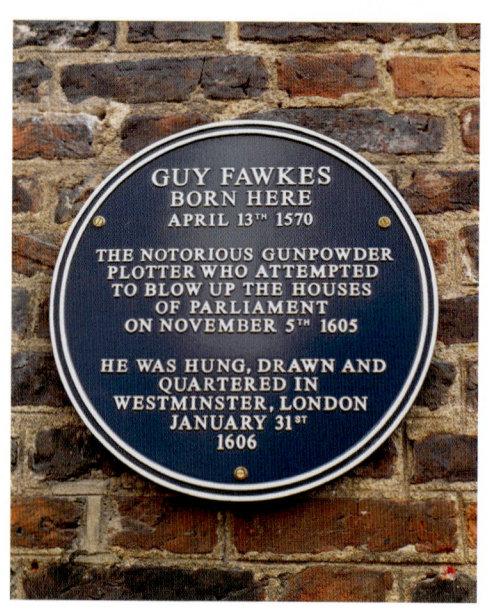

THE NORTH

PORTRAIT OF ENGLAND

MORNING PROMISE: Morning mist heralds another hot day in the Yorkshire Dales (opposite page).

An emerald patchwork of fields, punctuated with winter shelters for livestock, (bottom left) provides excellent grazing for the sheep (bottom right) and underpins the prosperity of the wool shops (top right) to be found all over the area.

THE NORTH

PORTRAIT OF ENGLAND

ILLUSTRIOUS SON: Explorer Captain Cook's statue (TOP LEFT) overlooks Whitby and the Abbey (OPPOSITE PAGE).

The young James Cook became a seaman after he moved to Staithes (BOTTOM LEFT) in 1744.

Heather tints the view across the North Yorkshire National Park (TOP RIGHT).

STORMY WATERS: The advent of cheap charter flights in the 1960's to Continental destinations offering guaranteed sunshine saw the decline of many of England's traditional holiday resorts. Blackpool (BELOW AND OPPOSITE PAGE) was no exception.

THE NORTH

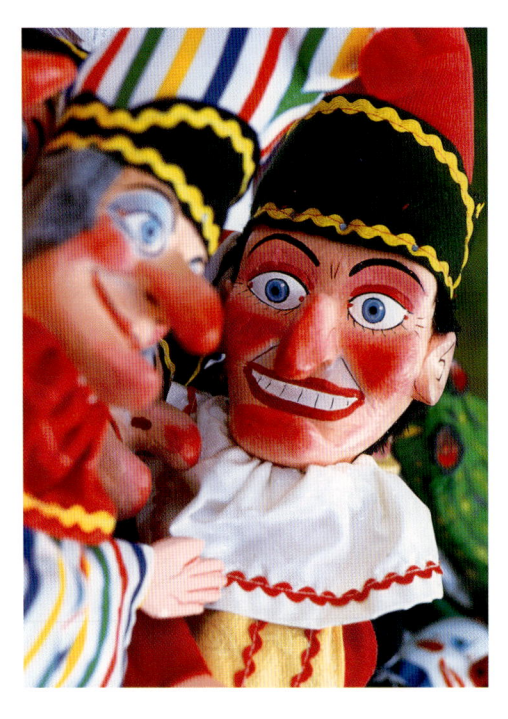

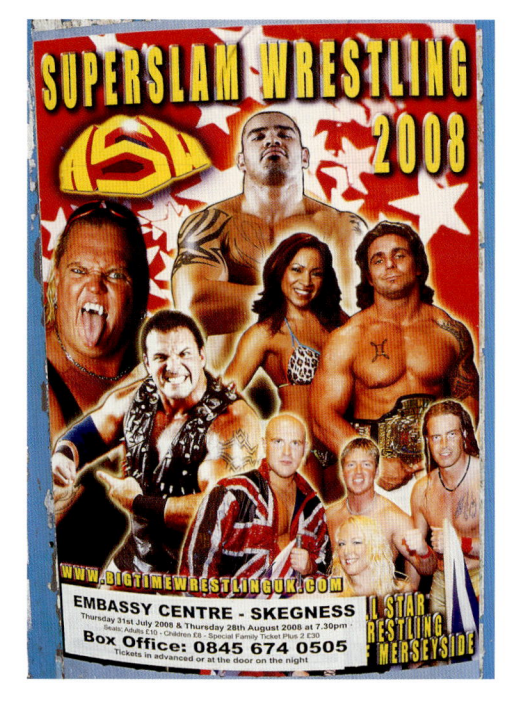

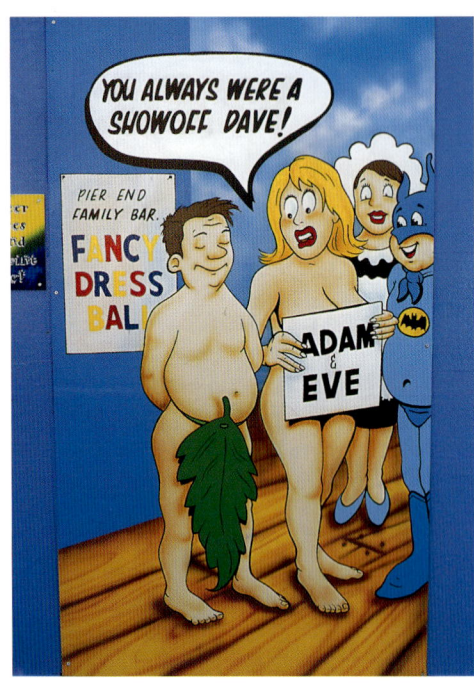

SIGNS OF THE TIMES: Timeless images that have remained unchanged for a century by the sea (ABOVE).

Resigned Skegness donkeys (OPPOSITE PAGE) await their next rides.

PORTRAIT OF ENGLAND

THE NORTH

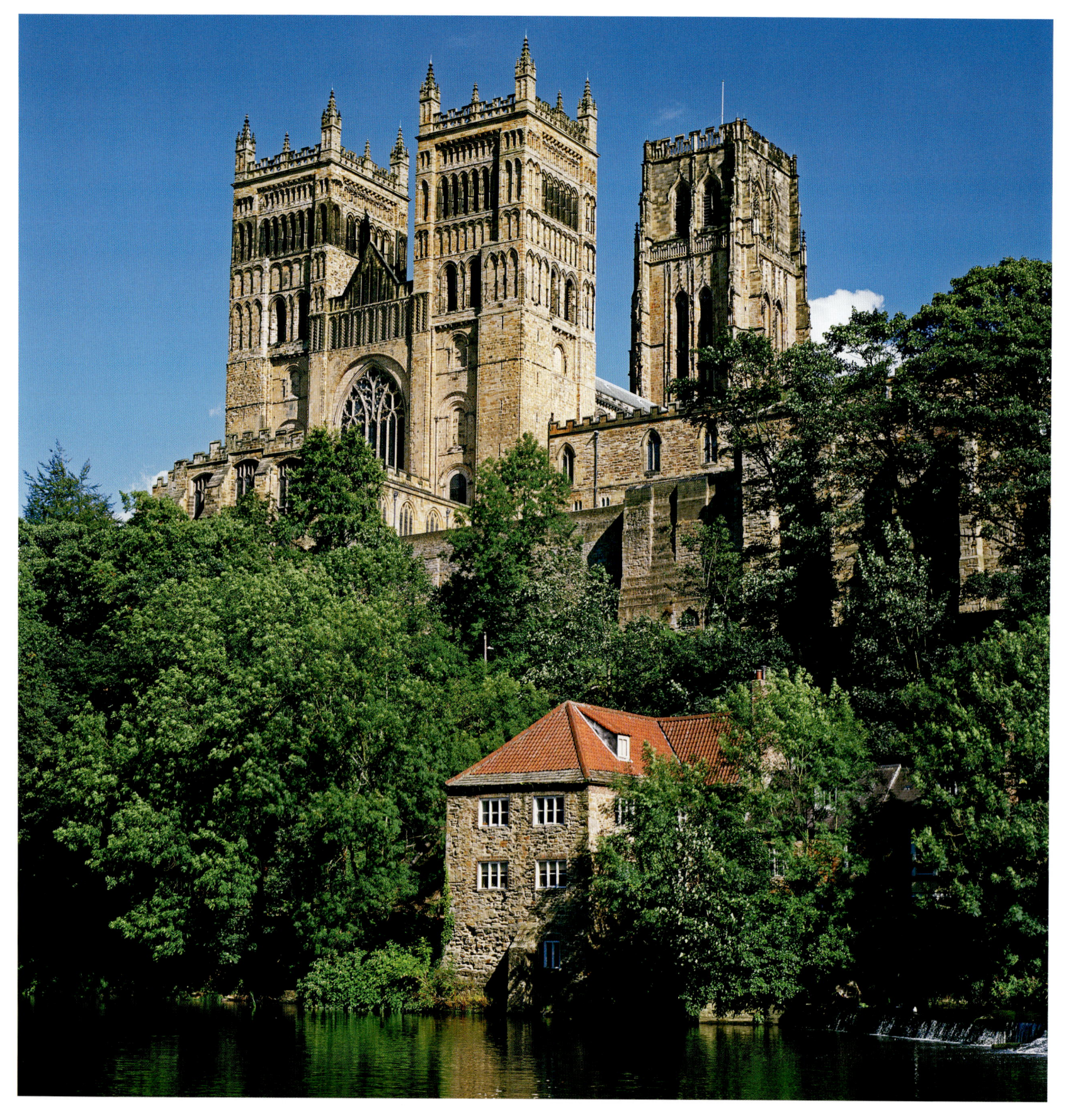

PORTRAIT OF ENGLAND

RELIGIOUS MASTERPIECE: Durham Cathedral is an unforgettable expression of religious belief that took 40 years to complete (OPPOSITE PAGE).

Beamish Open Air Museum in County Durham is a working museum which recreates how the people of the north lived and worked in the early eighteen and nineteen hundreds (THIS PAGE).

THE NORTH

CALM CONISTON: It's hard to imagine that Sir Donald Campbell's Bluebird broke the world water speed record on the flat calm surface of this idyllic lake (BOTTOM LEFT).

Windermere (TOP RIGHT) is England's largest lake at 10.5 miles long and a mile wide. But with 10,000 boats registered to sail there it can get busy.

Ambleside is the key centre for hikers on the 2,174 miles of rights of way in the Lake District. Bridge House (BOTTOM RIGHT) is the town's most eccentric attraction.

(OPPOSITE PAGE) Ashness Bridge near Keswick symbolizes the compact beauty of the region.

THE NORTH

PORTRAIT OF ENGLAND

LAKE WALK: The four and a half mile walk round Lake Buttermere makes an ideal afternoon's relaxation with a convenient pub serving as the finishing line (OPPOSITE PAGE).

Dove Cottage (LEFT) was poet William Wordsworth's home when he was enjoying his most productive period.

Derwentwater (BELOW) has featured in a number of classical novels.

THE NORTH

INVITING INN: The Three Shires Inn at Little Langdale (RIGHT) is built of slate and has always been a resting place for those tackling the Wrynose and Hardknott Passes.

A farm nestling below Little Langdale (BELOW).

Young visitors enjoy the view of Great Langdale and the Cumbrian Mountains (OPPOSITE PAGE).

THE NORTH

PORTRAIT OF ENGLAND

TYNE DUSK: The slender lines of the Gateshead Millennium Bridge have already received world-wide acclaim (OPPOSITE PAGE).

The Angel of the North (ABOVE), symbol of hope for the north-east, has already become one of the 12 icons of England.

BLUE MOOD: The dark hues of the Northumbrian countryside, with its areas of dark forest set against open moorland, are part of its appeal (BELOW).

Alnwick Castle (RIGHT) was restored by the dukes of Northumberland in the 18th and 19th centuries. Its latter day popularity soared when it was used as the setting for the Harry Potter movies.

Bamburgh Castle (OPPOSITE PAGE) was a prime target in the Wars of the Roses and was the first castle to succumb to cannon fire in 1464.

THE NORTH

HADRIAN'S DEFENCE: The remains of the 73.5 mile Hadrian's Wall (BOTTOM LEFT AND OPPOSITE PAGE) are best preserved in the vicinity of Housteads Fort (TOP RIGHT).

Re-enactment shows depict how a Roman Legionnaire would have looked (BOTTOM RIGHT).

(FOLLOWING PAGE) The sun breaks through over Northumbrian moorlands, a scene unchanged for hundreds of years.

THE NORTH

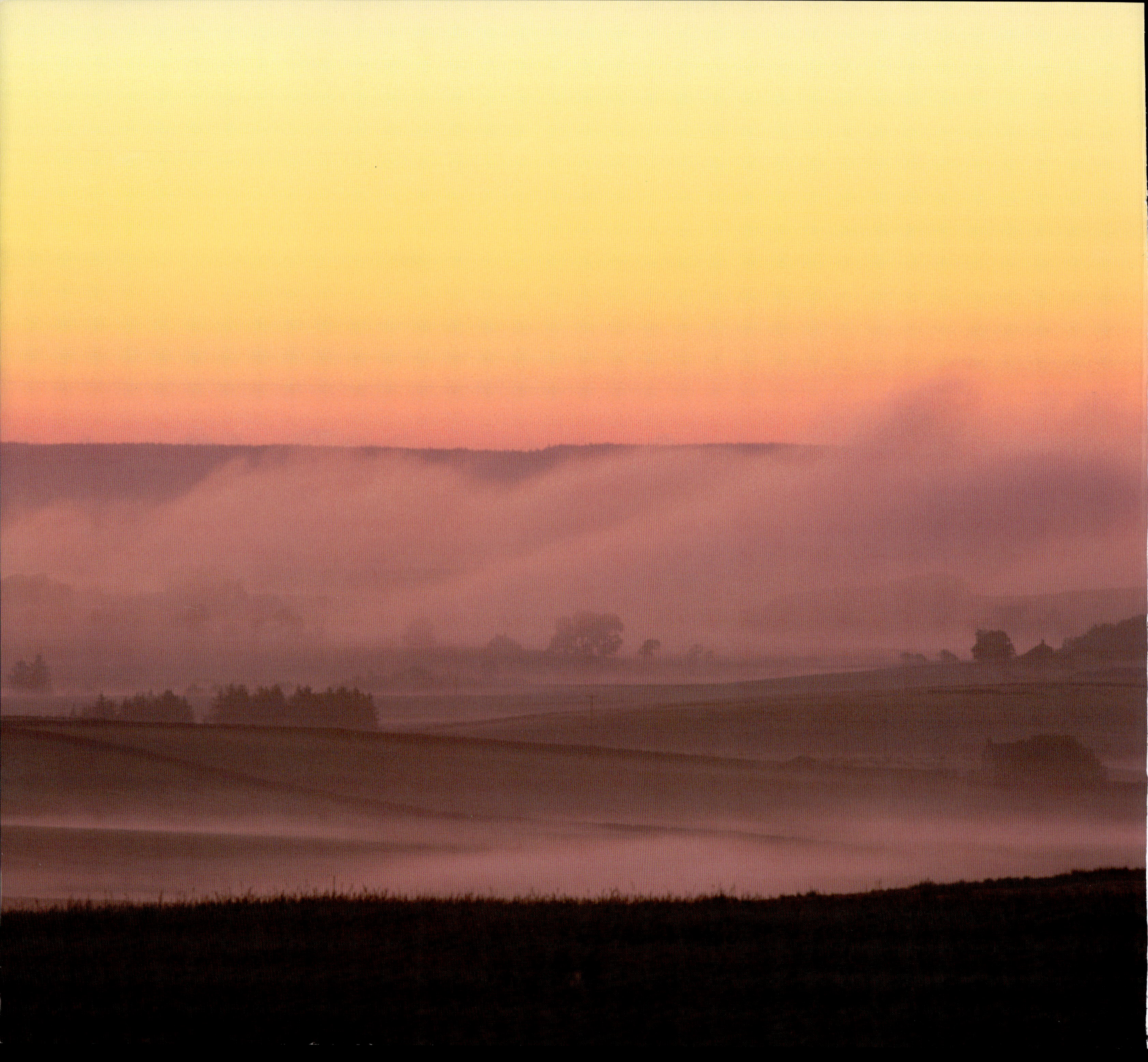